Science of Cycling

Edmund R. Burke, PhD
US Cycling Federation

Human Kinetics Books
Champaign, Illinois

Library of Congress Cataloging-in-Publication Data

Burke, Ed, 1949-
    Science of cycling.

    Bibliography: p.
    Includes index.
    1. Cycling—Training.   2. Bicycle racing.
    3. Cycling—Physiological aspects.   4. Cycling—
    Safety measures.   I. Title.
    GV1048.B87   1986   796.6   86-10246
    ISBN 0-87322-048-X
        0-87322-181-8 (pbk)

Developmental Editor: Sue Wilmoth, PhD
Production Director: Ernie Noa
Copy Editor: Jean Berry
Typesetter: Sandra Meier
Text Design: Julie Szamocki
Text Layout: Janet Davenport
Cover Design: Julie Szamocki
Cover Photo Courtesy of and Copyrighted by Dave Black © 1986
Photos in Chapter 2 Courtesy of Nancy Hobbs
Artwork in Chapter 8 by Stacy Kneeshaw
Printed by: United Graphics

ISBN: 0-87322-181-8 (paper)
        0-87322-048-X (cloth)

Copyright © 1986 by Edmund Burke

Printed in the United States of America

10   9   8   7   6   5

Published by Leisure Press
A Division of Human Kinetics
    Publishers
Box 5076,
Champaign, IL 61825-5076
1-800-747-4457

Canada Office:
Human Kinetics Publishers
P.O. Box 2503,
Windsor, ON N8Y 4S2
1-800-465-7301
    (in Canada only)

Europe Office:
Human Kinetics Publishers
    (Europe) Ltd.
P.O. Box IW14
Leeds LS16 6TR
England
0532-781708

Australia Office:
Human Kinetics Publishers
P.O. Box 80
Kingswood 5062
South Australia
374-0433

12-14-93

Contents

Acknowledgments

I am indebted to the many coaches, athletes, and researchers whose dedication to cycling made this book a reality. Without them our knowledge of cycling could not have advanced to the point where it is today.

I also wish to thank the U.S. Olympic Committee for its assistance in making this book possible through its funding of the Elite Athlete Program, which contributed to our success at the 1984 Olympic Games.

Preface

The role of science in cycling has grown over the past few years as more and more cyclists search for a competitive edge based on something more than long tradition or guesswork. No wonder then that many look to science to understand how and why certain things work and to sort out from their training regimens which methods are effective and which are not. This book is intended to provide a digest of the technical aspects of research that form the scientific basis for the concepts, both new and old, that affect the sport of cycling. Such an undertaking is sure to fall short of its mark, but if at best if offers some empirical basis for a cyclist to make decisions, it will have served its purpose.

In planning the book I sought a balance between the physiological, mechanical, biomechanical, psychological, and medical aspects of cycling. Chapter 1 gives the physiological parameters important to cycling in a way that is easy to understand and yet technically informative. Chapters 2 and 3 provide basic information on how weight training and stretching can improve performance. Because no work on cycling would be complete without a discussion of the biomechanical aspects, Robert Gregor and Peter Cavanagh discuss the effects of saddle height and pedaling mechanics to the biomechanical skill of cycling.

Reflecting the explosion of equipment design in cycling, Chester Kyle has contributed two chapters on the mechanical factors affecting cycling speed and equipment-design criteria. He shows how equipment can improve performance, efficiency, and ultimately results. Chapters 8 and 9 are devoted to the important topics of injury prevention and medical concerns. The final chapter deals with a new area of sport science, sport psychology. As far as I know, this is the first such discussion in a cycling handbook.

The altruistic commitment of the authors to the sharing of their knowledge and experience is commendable. Most of them are researchers and coaches currently working on research projects to improve the performance of our national and Olympic cycling teams. Their primary purpose is to present a broad and sound foundation on which the coach or cyclist can build his or her own program. Research at times ranges widely because the vertical height of cycling achievement is directly proportional to the horizontal foundation of knowledge on which it is based.

Not every cyclist or every coach can be a winner. The aim of this text is to provide a working base for improving performance levels.

Edmund R. Burke

CHAPTER 1

The Physiology of Cycling

Edmund Burke
US Cycling Federation, Center for Science, Medicine and Technology

Competitive cycling places certain demands on the physiological systems of the body. This chapter begins with how chemical energy is harnessed in muscle and how various training programs will provide the mechanical energy required for cycling. In particular the neuromuscular system, especially the muscle and nerves of the legs, experiences increased stress, the amount depending on the length and intensity of the ride. The cardiovascular system carries increased amounts of oxygen and nutrients to the working muscles. The heart rate may increase as much as threefold and the amount of blood pumped by the heart will rise from a resting level of 5 to 6 L/min to 20 to 30 L/min. The respiratory system will increase the amount of oxygen needed by increasing both the number of breaths per minute and the depth of each breath. If the cyclist and the coach want to make sound plans with respect to racing and training, they must first understand the physical demands placed upon the body and the changes produced over time.

Energy Expenditure

Few sports are as varied and physiologically demanding as competitive cycling. The races range from a 200 m match sprint that lasts approximately 11 s to the grueling Tour de France, which lasts 23 days and covers 5000 km. The Tour de France demands racing over high passes in the Alps with the possibility of sprints at the end of each stage. The body's adaption to the stress of riding is specific. Cyclists must train specifically for different events. Biochemically, an "impossible double" in cycling would be the sprints and road racing because the energy demands for these two events are different. Consider, then, the problems encountered by cyclists wanting to train to enter in a 100-mi road race. They must possess the aerobic potential for prolonged exertion and the anaerobic ability necessary for breaking away from the pack, climbing steep hills, and sprinting at the end of the race. Generally, cyclists tend to concentrate on similar events that demand similar energy sources. By recognizing which energy sources are being used during a given race, coaches may be able to prescribe the most effective conditioning program.

The relationship between different cycling events and the primary energy sources being utilized is shown in Table 1. For sprinters, the most important source is the breakdown of high-energy compounds called ATP (adenosinetriphosphate) and PC (phosphocreatine), the most available energy source of the muscle. One thousand meter cyclists and pursuiters, after using their immediate high-energy sources, obtain energy from the nonoxidative (anaerobic) breakdown of carbohydrates. Finally, long distance cyclists rely on the oxidative (aerobic) breakdown of carbohydrates and fats for energy. The point here is that the energy sources for a given event are time or distance dependent. The energy systems are linked to the particular distance and time the cyclist rides, thus illustrating the principle of specificity of training.

Table 1   Various Cycling Events and Their Predominant Energy Source

Event	Performance Time	Speed (ATP-PC Strength) (%)	Anaerobic Capacity (Speed and Lactic-Acid System) (%)	Aerobic Capacity (Oxygen System) (%)
	Hours and Mins.			
100 mi road race	3:55-4:10	—	5	95
100 km criterium	2:05-2:15	5	10	85
100 km team T.T.	2:10-2:20	—	15	85
25 mi T.	0:52-0:60	—	10	90
25 criterium	0:50-0:60	5	15	80
	Mins. and Secs.			
10 mi track	20:00-25:00	10	20	70
400 m individual pursuit	4:45- 5:05	20	55	25
Kilometer	1:07- 1:13	80	15	5
Match sprints	0:11- 0:13	98	2	—

Some of the percentages in the longer events may at first seem out of proportion. In a 100-mi road race lasting 4 hrs and 10 min, however, 5% of the total work energy is a considerable amount to be derived from anaerobic energy sources. Though the percentage is low, the anaerobic system must be developed to its optimum to work in the breaks, climb, and sprint at the conclusion of the competition. Table 2 gives an approximation of the total energy yield from both aerobic and anaerobic processes during maximal efforts of up to 120-min duration for an individual with high maximal aerobic power. With work time up to 2 min, the anaerobic power is most important; at about 2 min, a 50:50 ratio exists; as the time increases, aerobic power becomes more important.

Table 2 Relative Contribution of Total Energy Yield From Aerobic and Anaerobic Energy Processes During Maximal Efforts Up to 120 Min

Energy Source		Exercise Time, Maximal Effort						
	10 S	1 Min	2 Min	4 Min	10 Min	30 Min	60 Min	120 Min
Anaerobic	85	65-70	50	30	10-15	5	2	1
Aerobic	15	30-35	50	70	85-90	95	98	99

Energy Transformation

As discussed previously, the cyclist has two main metabolic pathways for producing energy: with oxygen (aerobically) or without oxygen (anaerobically). The main source of energy for distance cycling is supplied aerobically. Long-distance cycling uses fats and carbohydrates as the fuels to produce energy. Fat stores play a greater role as the distance of the event increases. The body can store about 2,000 kcal of carbohydrates (glycogen) and about 50,000 to 70,000 kcal of fats. Prolonged, easy riding (a load requiring about 70% or less of the cyclist's maximum) can be sustained almost entirely from the burning of fats. As the intensity of the effort increases, more and more carbohydrates are required. Consequently, during long hard road races, muscle glycogen is an important fuel. In fact, one of the causes of the *bonk* may be linked to muscle-glycogen depletion.

Some indication exists that the ability of cyclists to use fats as a fuel is related to their $\dot{V}O_2$max (the maximum amount of oxygen the body can use per minute). This may be because, at a given workload, a cyclist with a lower $\dot{V}O_2$max will produce more lactic acid (waste product of anaerobic exercise) than a cyclist with a higher $\dot{V}O_2$max.

High levels of blood lactic acid may interfere with the release of fats. Research has also shown that trained skeletal muscle has a greater capacity to use fats. The increased capacity to use fats, combined with the increased ability of trained cyclists to release fats from adipose tissue, suggests that training enhances the proportion of energy that can be produced through fat metabolism.

The question becomes, how can cyclists train themselves to use fat efficiently as a source of fuel? The answer is simple. Every time they go out on a 3 to 4 hr training ride, they are training their bodies to burn fat as the main source of fuel as the ride progresses. A highly trained cyclist, while racing, can ride at a lower percentage of his or her $\dot{V}O_2$max, which will allow him or her to burn a higher percentage of fat than the less-conditioned rider with a low $\dot{V}O_2$max.

Anaerobic metabolism depends on muscle glycogen and blood glucose as its fuel for work. Lactic acid is the end product of this system. Without oxygen the glucose or stored glycogen breaks down into lactic acid. If sufficient oxygen were present, the breakdown of glucose would continue into aerobic metabolism. At high lactic-acid levels, muscular contraction is inhibited. This occurs because the proteins in the muscle cells can function only within a certain range of acidity. Excess lactic acid shuts down the reactions taking place within the cell. The result is fatigue; either the exercise must be stopped or its intensity greatly reduced. Anaerobic metabolism cannot support exercise for extended periods and hence is considered of little importance in distance cycling as long as the pace is steady and the sprint is not too long.

What effect does training have on the muscle's production of and tolerance to lactic acid? Training increases the cellular components responsible for aerobic work. After training at any submaximal workload cyclists will produce less lactate than when they were untrained (i.e., their aerobic capacity was greater). The body is able to use oxygen more efficiently and the muscles tolerate more lactic acid.

Training to improve anaerobic capacity involves repetitive rides of nearly all-out effort of from 10 s to 1-1/2 min. Riding much further would require holding back, and the benefit of the workout in increasing speed and anaerobic capacity would be reduced. Relief intervals should be a minimum of 3 min to allow the lactate to diffuse out of the muscles. The relief interval should include light pedaling. During recovery, lactic acid is more rapidly removed and resynthesized by light exercise than by rest. This allows a more rapid distribution of the lactate to the liver and other muscles. The liver and resting muscles can change the lactate back into glucose to be used immediately or to be stored as glycogen.

Training Programs

The different types of training to stress the metabolic systems will be described here briefly and can be adapted to the individual needs of the cyclists. Table 3 shows the approximate percentage of contribution to the energy system that is possible through each of eight training methods. Table 1 can be used with Table 2 in planning workouts. If a cyclist is training for several events, a combination of several programs can be used to increase performance.

Table 3 Contribution of Training Programs
to the Development of Energy Sources

Type of Training	ATP-PC and LA (%)	LA and Aerobic (%)	Aerobic Capacity (%)
Sprint training	90	6	4
Acceleration sprints	90	5	5
Set sprints	30	50	20
Intervals	10-30	30-50	20-60
Speed play (fartlek)	20	40	40
Repetition riding	10	50	40
Continuous fast riding	2	13	85
Continuous slow riding		5	95

Sprint Training

Sprint training requires the repetition of short sprints as a means of preparation for competitive cycling. This means riding at maximum speed, an all-out effort, for 75 to 100 m with relatively long rest periods.

Acceleration Sprints

Acceleration sprints involve a gradual increase from a slow steady pace to an all-out effort: one-third easy effort, one-third medium-hard effort and one-third maximum effort, for about 200 to 250 m. This type of training will increase both speed and endurance if enough repetitions are used. This program is valuable in cold weather because the cyclist gradually reaches top speed and avoids risk of muscle injury.

Set Sprints

A set of sprints followed by a rest period of recovery riding will develop speed and endurance. A typical program might be: sprint 75 m, medium pace for 75 m, sprint 75 m, very slow 75 m for recovery prior to next set; sprint 100, medium 100, sprint 100, slow 100 before next repetition; sprint 150, medium 150, sprint 150; repeat program when totally recovered.

Intervals

Interval training involves riding a series of repeat efforts at a given distance with a controlled number of rest periods. Rest intervals will allow partial recovery of heart rate to normal. *Slow interval training* is used for endurance fitness and does not contribute much to speed. It requires riding repeat distance at slower-than-race pace with short recovery periods. An example would be 25 × 750 m with 30-s rest intervals at a pace that would bring the heart rate to 170 to 175 beats/min. *Fast interval training* involves longer rest periods, greater recovery of heart rate to normal, and a faster riding pace. An example would be 20 × 750 to 1000 m with 120-s rest interval. A good training heart rate would be 180 to 185 beats/min. This helps cyclists withstand fatigue in the absence of oxygen.

Speed Play

Basically speed play uses all of the training methods described in this article. The term is commonly used in running; the more common Swedish name is "fartlek," which means riding fairly long distances using a variety of speeds. It can be done on a velodrome or on the roads. Speed play is psychologically stimulating, when used properly, and will develop both training capacities. An example would be:

1. Warm-up 5 mi
2. 5 × 100 m fast, 60 s rest
3. 5 mi, 3/4 effort
4. 4 to 6 × 100 m acceleration sprints: easy 25, medium 50, hard 25, and easy 10 after each

5. 4 to 6 × 750 to 1000 m faster than race pace, and easy 1000 after each
6. Medium pace 5 mi
7. 8 to 10 × 75 to 100 m, 7/8 effort, easy 250 m between
8. 1/2 to 3/4 effort 10 mi
9. 4 to 6 short hill sprints, easy ride back down
10. Warm-down for 3 to 5 mi

This fast-slow riding is physiologically best for the middle distance to distance riding.

Repetition Riding

The cyclist rides a set distance at a fast speed (close to race pace) with the rest periods long enough to allow almost complete recovery. Usually repetition riding is used with riding longer distances than interval training (2,000 to 1,000 m). The longer the distance, the slower the cyclist rides. A 4,000 m cyclist may ride at his or her race pace or a few seconds slower for 2,000 m with complete recovery between efforts.

Continuous Slow Riding

The program that involves riding long distances at speeds slower than race pace is called continuous slow riding. The distance covered will be related to the racer's event. A sprinter may need to ride only 25 mi while a road cyclist may cover 125 mi in one training session. This type of training, highly recommended by Dr. Ernst Van Aaken, may better be known as long slow distance (LSD). The heart rate is about 150 beats/min, and no times need be kept. The greatest increase is in aerobic endurance.

Continuous Fast Riding

Continuous fast riding is different from slow riding in the speed of the ride. Distance is not quite as long as slow continuous riding but longer than race distance. As an example, a woman cyclist whose race distance is 3,000 m may ride 3,500 to 4,000 m several times, with a 5 to 10 min rest period. Again, this type of workout is good for endurance training and gradually conditions the body to the race pace.

The Cardiorespiratory System

The lungs and lung volumes of trained athletes are larger than those of untrained individuals. These changes may be the result of increased strength of the muscle used in breathing or the fact that athletes themselves are slightly larger. Whatever the cause, little correlation exists between athletic performance and lung volume. More important than lung volume may be the cyclist's $\dot{V}O_2$max. The greatest amount of oxygen that can be used during all-out cycling is generally considered the best single indicator of the cardiorespiratory system's functional capacity. The greater the rate of oxygen delivery to the tissues, the greater the rate of work that can be maintained.

Aerobic power is known to improve with training. The magnitude of improvement is usually 15% to 20%. The type and amount of training as well as genetic capabilities that are passed on from the cyclist's parents (e.g., muscle fiber type) greatly affect aerobic capacity. Many researchers consider the level of aerobic capacity to be the limiting factor in the endurance exercise. Like many other trained endurance athletes, road cyclists possess exceptionally high $\dot{V}O_2$max values. Table 4 compares the maximal oxygen consumption values for cyclists as reported by several investigators.

The $\dot{V}O_2$max values for individual cyclists as recorded in the literature are shown in Table 5. Cyclists 1 and 2 were professionals in

Table 4   Team $\dot{V}O_2$max Data (Mean ± SD)

Study	Number of Subjects	$\dot{V}O_2$max $(ml \cdot kg^{-1} \cdot min^{-1})$	Notes
Saltin	6	74.0	1966 Swedish national team
Hermansen	16	73.0	Norwegian national team
Burke	11	67.1	National class road and track cyclists
Stromme	5	69.1	1975 Swedish national team
Present study			
Men's national team	23	74.0 ± 8.3	
Category 1 men	8	70.6 ± 9.5	
Junior national team	15	64.8 ± 5.5	
Women's national team	6	57.4 ± 6.6	

Table 5 Individual $\dot{V}O_2$max Values

Study	Cyclist	$\dot{V}O_2$max (ml·kg^{-1}·min^{-1})	Notes
Stromme	1	77.0	5-time winner of Tour de France
Saltin	2	80.0	1970 winner of Tour of Italy
Burke	3	82.7	1975, 1979 Pan-American road team, 1976 Olympic road team
Burke	4	79.8	1972, 1976 Olympic road team, 1976, 1977 national road champion, 1975, 1979 Pan-American road team

Europe. The other cyclists were world-class amateurs. Well-trained cyclists apparently have the metabolic characteristics of high-caliber, endurance-trained athletes. Over a 3-year period the $\dot{V}O_2$max of the third cylcist was 79.6, 82.8, and 82.2 ml · kg^{-1} · min^{-1}, and his maximal heart rate was 187, 189, and 189 beats/min^{-1}.

The mean value for $\dot{V}O_2$max in the women's team is considerably higher than that found for the average woman (Table 4). When compared to values for other women athletes, the present values are also high. Hermansen (1973) reported a mean value of 3.65 L/min^{-1} for six Norwegian women orienteers, reportedly the best orienteers in Norway at the time, which is comparable to the 3.58 L/min^{-1} for the six women tested in this study. Orienteers have demonstrated consistently higher mean $\dot{V}O_2$max values than any other sport. The values reported for the juniors (4.45 L/min^{-1}) are higher than those reported by Placheta and Drazil (1971) for trained 17- to 18-year-old male cyclists (3.79 L/min^{-1}). Analysis of variance for maximal oxygen consumption showed a significant difference only between the men's and junior national teams (Table 4).

The small metabolic differences between the men's national team and Category 1 cyclists are of interest. Factors such as anaerobic threshold and efficiency may play an important role in cycling, as has been shown to be the case for other athletes. On the other hand, a difference of only 3.4 ml · kg^{-1} · min^{-1} for $\dot{V}O_2$max, although far from significant, may represent an advantage in high-level competition.

Foster and Daniels (1975) studied 16 competitive cyclists representing different senior categories and found a direct relationship between performance ability and mean aerobic power. This suggests that the general level of performance by competitive cyclists largely depends on aerobic power. Muscle-fiber composition and enzyme activity, however, do not seem to influence success in competitive cycling. Burke,

Cerny, Costill, and Fink (1977) found no significant difference between classifications of trained senior cyclists, although they found differences in $\dot{V}O_2$max.

The mean values for the junior national team, while significantly different from the senior team, are comparable to the values reported for Category 1 men in Table 4. This characteristic profile of the juniors and seniors can be seen in actual head-to-head competition, in which the juniors compete to acquire skill and experience. They have no problem placing well among the Category 1 men, but only a few can challenge the senior men's team.

Although $\dot{V}O_2$max may be an indicator of success in competitive cycling, separating cause from effect is always difficult. Is the athlete successful because of specific oxygen consumption or is oxygen consumption a result of training for the sport? Unless combined with other criteria, $\dot{V}O_2$max may be useful primarily in making relatively gross separations of talent. Still, a high $\dot{V}O_2$max is one of the characteristics of a competitive cyclist.

Aerobic power improves with training, as was noted earlier. The magnitude of improvement (usually 15% to 20%) is far less, however, than the differences among the categories (25% to 30%). For example, a Category 3 rider with a $\dot{V}O_2$max of about 50 ml/kg probably had a $\dot{V}O_2$max of about 50 ml/kg before training. A Category 1 rider with about 70 ml/kg aerobic power must have had an aerobic power of about 58 ml/kg before training. Because aerobic power shows most of its improvement with relatively modest training (see Figure 1), the greater volume and intensity of training done by the better riders would not be reason for the differences in aerobic power among the categories.

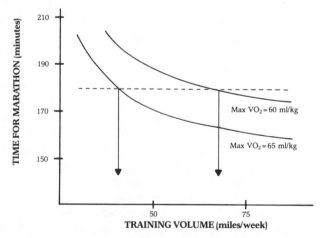

Figure 1   Relationship of training volume to marathon performance for individuals with $\dot{V}O_2$max equal to 60 and 65 ml/kg respectively. Note the greater amount of training required to run a 3-hour marathon in the less "talented" runner.

We have answered one question by posing another: What factors allow some individuals to develop more aerobic power than others? The factors limiting aerobic power are still subject to debate among exercise physiologists; however, most agree that the maximal cardiac output or the greatest amount of blood the heart can pump per minute is a factor of great importance in determining aerobic power. Athletes (including cyclists) with great aerobic power have also been shown to have great values for cardiac output (Ekblom & Hermansen, 1968). The difference between individuals with large values for cardiac output and those with more nominal values appears to be primarily a function of the amount of blood that can be pumped with each beat (stroke volume). This suggests that the size of the heart might be inherently greater in some individuals than in others, which is not unlikely when one considers the great range of variation noted in the size of other anatomical features. If tall individuals have a natural advantage in basketball and large individuals dominate in football, why might not those with large hearts dominate in endurance sports (cycling, running, Nordic skiing)?

Does this mean that only cyclists whose aerobic power is above 70 ml/kg will reach Category 1? The answer is both no and yes. The range of variation within a category is large. I have tested Category 3 riders above 65 ml/kg and Category 1 riders as low as 60 ml/kg, which proves that relatively great aerobic power is no assurance of success. It also suggests, however, the existence of some functional lower limit for aerobic power necessary to break into Category 1. A given individual has relatively great variation in performance as more and more training is done, even though that individual's aerobic power may not change.

Figure 1 presents some data recently obtained for marathon runners. I believe that the principle expressed applies equally well to cyclists. As may be seen, runners with lower aerobic power may perform at the same level as more "talented" runners as a result of a greater volume of training. Within certain limits a highly motivated cyclist with less than optimal talent may perform well. This secondary training effect is probably a function of changes in the muscle tissue and is currently at the forefront of much research in exercise physiology.

The Neuromuscular System

Cycling is coordinated interaction between the nervous and muscular systems. The muscles of the legs are composed of bundles of muscle fibers, all of which function basically in the same way; that is, when stimulated they contract and develop tension to turn the pedals around.

Two main types of muscle fibers can be distinguished. Fibers that are able to contract repeatedly when stimulated, without fatigue, are called slow-twitch fibers. These fibers have a high content of myoglobin (an oxygen-storing protein) and high aerobic capacity. A cell's aerobic capacity is its ability to produce energy at a steady rate when sufficient oxygen is available. Slow-twitch fibers have a large number of mitochondria, those components of the cell that contain all the necessary oxidative enzymes. The slow-twitch fiber develops tension gradually, reaching peak tension slowly. Slow-twitch fibers are used primarily during long-distance cyling.

The other major fiber type found in human skeletal muscle is fast-twitch. These fibers have a lesser amount of myoglobin, and a rather low mitochondrial volume, giving them a lower amount of aerobic enzymes. This fiber develops tension rather fast and derives its energy from anaerobic metabolism. These two fiber types also have different capacities for breaking down glycogen (stored carbohydrate) and accumulating lactate. In other words, they have different anaerobic capacities, that is, the ability of the cells to produce energy quickly, but only for a short time, when sufficient oxygen is not available. The fast-twitch fiber has the highest anaerobic capacity and is thus able to perform short-term, very intense work.

Not all fibers that are slow twitch and not all fibers that are fast twitch have identical characteristics, however. A spectrum of aerobic and anaerobic potentials exists within both types. One person's fast-twitch fibers may have a greater aerobic capacity than another person's fast-twitch fibers. In a given muscle, however, a person's slow-twitch fibers will usually have a higher aerobic capacity than the fast-twitch fibers. The reverse is true for anaerobic capacity. The primary reason for emphasizing this is that different training regimens can enhance the aerobic or anaerobic capacity of the muscle fiber. A cyclist training for long distance riding may have a higher aerobic capacity in the fast-twitch fibers of the legs than in the slow-twitch fibers of the arms.

In the average population the relative muscle fiber composition is 40% to 50% slow twitch and 50% to 60% fast twitch. An interesting point is that, within the same individual, very small variations appear to exist in fiber composition from one muscle to another. The only muscle that distinguishes itself from all others is the soleus muscle (a calf muscle), which in humans is mainly composed of slow-twitch fibers. Between individuals, however, certain variations in muscle-fiber composition are found.

Traits of Highly Successful Cyclists

A study (Burke, 1977) was conducted to determine if highly successful cyclists can be distinguished from less successful yet highly trained cyclists on the basis of selected muscle and aerobic characteristics. Twenty-two male and seven female competitive cyclists were used as subjects. The male competitive cyclists were further separated on the basis of success in national and/or international competition. Group A consisted of 11 cyclists who had won some national and/or international competitions. The remaining 11 males had no outstanding race achievements to their credit. The female cyclists, while of varying abilities, were treated as one group because of the small number of subjects.

Physical characteristics of the cyclists in the study are shown in Table 6. When compared to Group B, the A group showed significantly higher $\dot{V}O_2$max. The aerobic data on the females is comparable to that found in other highly trained females tested on a bicycle ergometer. Although the mean $\dot{V}O_2$max for Group A (67 ml/kg/min) is not as high as that reported for endurance-trained runners, several factors may be involved. $\dot{V}O_2$max recorded on a bicycle ergometer are 5% to 8% lower than when recorded on a treadmill. During running more muscle mass is used and, as a consequence, more oxygen is needed. In addition, the majority of the subjects were tested in the early stages of training. Two of the cyclists who were later retested in the competitive season were found to have increased their $\dot{V}O_2$max values.

Table 6   Mean ($\pm$ S.E.) Characteristics of Trained Male and Female Cyclists and Untrained Men and Women

Subjects	Sex	Age (yr)	Height (cm)	Weight (kg)	VO$_2$max (ml/kg·min)	Years of Competition	ST %
Cyclist A	M	24.6 (3.5)	180.0 (1.0)	72.8 (1.4)	67.1 (1.8)	5.6 (2.0)	56.8 (4.4)
Cyclist B	M	24.5 (1.6)	175.4 (1.0)	70.4 (2.3)	57.1 (2.9)	3.1 (0.8)	53.3 (5.1)
Cyclist	F	20.1 (3.1)	165.0 (1.8)	55.0 (2.1)	50.2 (2.9)	4.2 (1.3)	50.5 (5.4)

The percentage of slow-twitch (ST) fibers in the three groups of trained cyclists was not significantly different (see Table 6). A fiber composition of approximately 50% FT and 50% ST may be of benefit in cycling because most cycling events involve both endurance and sprinting abilities. This point is well documented in Table 7. Sheila Young-Ochowicz, for example, possesses 47% ST and was World Champion in both sprint cycling and speed skating. Sheila was a skater first and a cyclist second. Even her shortest event, the 500 m, was not a true sprint, because it lasted 40+ s.

The observations reported in Table 6 demonstrate that

1. the groups of male and female cyclists show similar muscle-fiber composition;
2. an extremely high percentage of slow-twitch or fast-twitch fiber composition is not a requirement for success in competitive road cycling; and
3. $\dot{V}O_2$max is a good predictor of competitive success at the present time.

Table 7   V Groups "A," "B," and Women Cyclists:
Characteristics of Selected Subjects

Group	Subject	Age (Years)	Slow-Twitch Fibers %	$\dot{V}O_2$max (ml/kg)
A	Doughty, T.*	22	31	69.0
A	Stetina, D.*	19	64	72.6
A	Stetina, W.*	22	60	69.2
B	Nichols, E.*	19	64	58.4
B	Prall, B.*	24	67	60.1
B	Tripp, J.*	26	48	60.8
Women	Young-Ochowicz, S.*	25	47	55.0
Women	Olpolski, K.*	18	50	—
Women	Paraskevin, C.*	14	37	49.6

*Written permission was obtained to identify these subjects. These data were measured in 1975.

It should be noted that most of the subjects were road riders, and an "ideal" muscle-fiber composition may be beneficial for certain events. To predict what pure match sprinters need is rather easy. They should be endowed with a high percentage of fast-twitch fibers (as reported for Connie Paraskevin, 1982 World Sprint Champion). With weight and sprint training they can enhance the strength and anaerobic capacity of these fibers.

In summary, a high percentage of fast-twitch fibers is ideal for the match sprinter (or kilometer) cyclist. A muscle-fiber composition of 70% to 80% slow-twitch fibers is ideal for endurance riding, but a cyclist could be fairly sure to succeed only in long time trialing and stage racing. The fiber-typing technique has been used strictly as a research tool for the studies described here. Although a significantly high population of a particular fiber type can enhance athletic success, data from a single sample could be misleading or psychologically damaging to a cyclist if the findings were not deemed desirable. Scientists should not be in the business of predicting success. Other measurements that can yield valuable information relating to athletic potential include strength, aerobic and anaerobic capacity, peak lactate concentrations in blood after maximal efforts, and years of experience.

Nutritional Considerations

The search for ways to improve performance has taken cyclists down many roads. The preoccupation with winning, prestige, and peer approval frequently causes cyclists to follow poor advice on nutrition. The conclusion of most authors who have reviewed the relationship between nutritional status and physical performance is that a well-balanced diet is enough to ensure optimal performance. Attention to proper nutrition is important to athletes because deficiencies in calories, nutrients, or water can lower performance.

The main source of energy during cycling is derived from the metabolism of fats and carbohydrates, as was noted earlier. During moderate cycling, energy is supplied to active muscles by fat and glycogen. The increased capacity of trained cyclists to utilize fats, combined with their ability to release free fatty acids from adipose tissue, has already been discussed.

Although fat stores are greater than carbohydrates, and fat contains more energy per gram, the generation of this energy through aerobic metabolism requires more oxygen. During cycling, the consumption of 1 L of oxygen burning pure carbohydrate yields 5 kcal of energy compared to 4.7 kcal when fat is burned. This makes the metabolism of carbohydrate 7% to 8% more efficient than fat, and hence carbohydrates are the preferred substrate during heavy work loads when the efficiency of energy production is important. For example, a work load that requires 4 L of oxygen to complete with carbohydrates would require 4.4 L of oxygen when utilizing fat.

A shift to carbohydrate utilization during heavy cycling is a distinct advantage to the cyclist, because at this level of work, efficient utilization of oxygen is important to performance. At low and medium work loads, oxygen-delivery capabilities are not greatly taxed and more than sufficient oxygen is available for cycling. As the pace of the race increases, the capacity to deliver oxygen is near maximum and the metabolism of a larger percentage of carbohydrate results in a greater energy yield per unit of oxygen consumed.

In recent years it has been found that glycogen stores can be greatly increased when a high-carbohydrate diet is introduced during the few days preceding competition, commonly known as carbohydrate loading. Approximately three days before a big race, the cyclist switches to a diet high in carbohydrate—about 80% of total caloric intake. The diet should contain ample amounts of protein and fat. The high-carbohydrate diet is then maintained until the day of competition. In this way the glycogen stores in the muscles can be increased severalfold.

Hoping to increase body size and strength, many cyclists have used high-protein diets and supplements. This blind belief in protein goes back to ancient times, when athletes ate raw meat hoping to increase their own muscle mass. Actually the basic diet provides optimal protein. A diet that includes dairy products, soy products, and meats will contain enough high-quality protein. The many functions that proteins perform in the body can be met with a daily intake of 0.8 g/kg body weight (2.2 lb), because protein is not used as a fuel for exercise. An individual weighing 150 lb thus needs about 55 g of protein a day, or about 15% of the total caloric intake. The average diet contains 3 to 4 times the protein required for optimal performance. In addition, the major portion of protein intake is in the form of meat, which contains large amounts of saturated fats and cholesterol, two substances already eaten in excess. Most of the excess protein is converted into fat by the liver and stored in the adipose tissues of the body, thereby failing to perform any of its basic functions.

The area in which faddism, misconception, and ignorance are most obvious among cyclists concerns vitamin, mineral, and fluid intake. We all have heard reports that the use of vitamins, minerals, and other food supplements can give the cyclist a "winning edge." Although the use of many types of drugs is illegal, no restrictions exist against vitamin and mineral supplements. Vitamins and minerals are constituents of food and are essential for sustaining life and a healthy body.

Vitamins

Vitamins are divided into two groups: those soluble in fat and those soluble in water. Vitamins A, D, E, and K are in the first group, whereas C and B complex vitamins are water soluble. Solubility is important in determining whether the body can store a vitamin or whether it needs to be supplied daily. It also determines its toxicity potential when taken in large amounts.

If a cyclist does not have enough B and C vitamins, a decline in performance will be seen in a few weeks. These vitamins are needed for the production of energy and are not stored in the body to any significant degree. When the intake is greater than the body needs, the excess is excreted in the urine. Excess fat-soluble vitamins, on the other hand, are stored in the liver and fatty tissues of the body. If stores have been accumulated over a long period of time, an athlete may get along on inadequate amounts for several weeks.

Cyclists may decide to supplement their diets with B and C vitamins to ensure an adequate supply. Although this is probably not necessary if they eat a balanced diet of fresh foods, B or C supplements will not be harmful. The labels on the products provide the needed information. Excessive ingestion of certain fat-soluble vitamins, however, may result in toxicity.

Minerals

Minerals are important regulators of physiological processes involved in physical performance. They are considered in two groups: those present in relatively large amounts in the body and those needed in small quantities (the trace elements).

The major minerals are needed in levels greater than 100 mg/day and include calcium, phosphorus, magnesium, sodium, potassium, and chloride. The trace minerals comprise 17 substances that have biological functions, although the Food and Nutrition Board of the National Research Council has recognized only 10. These include fluorine, chromium, manganese, cobalt, copper, iron, zinc, selenium, molybdenum, and iodine. Mineral supplements are not needed by a hard-training cyclist. In hot weather, when sweat losses may be greater, an increase in salt intake will replace the sodium and chloride that may be lost in sweat.

Water Intake

During competition and training many athletes underestimate the importance of water, which is one of the six basic nutrients along with carbohydrate, fat, protein, vitamins, and minerals. While on a 50- to 75-mi race on a hot day with only two water bottles, a rider may lose from 7 to 10 lb of water weight. The water in both bottles (approximately 40 oz) will replace only 2-1/2 lb of lost fluid. Such losses put severe demands on the circulatory system, which is approximately 70% water.

When water is lost, plasma (the water portion of blood) has a limited capacity to carry nutrients (e.g., glucose, fats, oxygen) to the working muscles and to remove the byproducts of metabolism (e.g., carbon dioxide, heat, and lactic acid). Although it may be impossible to offset all water lost in sweating, even partial replacement can limit the problems of overheating and minimize the threat of circulatory collapse. The three rules a cyclist should follow while training or racing in hot weather are

1. drink 13 to 20 oz of fluid 15 min before riding;
2. drink several oz of fluid (0.2 L) every 10 to 15 min during the ride; and
3. keep a chart on morning weight and avoid getting into a state of chronic dehydration.

Thirst is not always a good indicator of the needs for fluids. In hot weather plenty of fluids should be drunk between meals and in the evening. A fluid of less than 2.5% simple sugar or about 7% of a carbohydrate polymer appears to be the most appropriate during exercise. If higher glucose concentrations are ingested, the rate of absorption goes down; the advantage of greater glucose concentration is then offset by lack of gastric emptying into the intestine where it can be absorbed into the blood stream.

Summary

This chapter has highlighted the responses of the cyclist's physiology to training and competition. Although the endurance cyclist's physiological capacity is limited by the ability to deliver oxygen to the working muscles, marked individual variations appear to exist in cycling efficiency, muscle-fiber types, and other factors. They are of major importance in a winning performance. The chapter also has provided information in the important area of nutrition, fluid replacement, and vitamin supplementation.

The objective of every cycling coach should be to develop the ultimate natural potential of each cyclist. This is compatible with the goals of the sport scientist. Unlike the trial-and-error methods of traditional coaching, an understanding of the physiological demands of cycling will provide cyclists with information that allows them to take best advantage of their innate capacities.

References

Burke, E.R., Cerny, R., Costill, D., & Fink, W. (1977). Characteristics of skeletal muscle in competitive cyclists. *Medicine and Science in Sports, 9*(2), 109-112.

Burke, E.R. (1980). Physiological characteristics of national and international competitive cyclists. *Physician and Sports Medicine, 8*(6), 78-84.

Ekblom, B., & Hermansen, L. (1968). Cardiac output in athletes. *Journal of Applied Physiology, 25*, 619.

Foster, C., & Daniels, J. (1975). Aerobic power of competitive cyclists. *Australian Journal of Sports Medicine, 7*(5), 111-112.

Hermansen, L. (1973). Oxygen transport during exercise in human subjects. *Acta Physiologica Scandinavica, 399* (Suppl.), 1-104.

Placheta, Z., & Drazil, V. (1971). Application of long-term medical examination results to the training system of cyclists. *Journal of Sports Medicine and Physical Fitness, 11*, 52-58.

CHAPTER 2

Strength Training for Cycling

Harvey Newton
National Weight Lifting Coach, 1981-1984

Strength training for cyclists has been a controversial topic for the past few years. Most other sports are accepting the need for weight training more readily. Within the past year, several authors have discussed the merits of weight training for more efficient cycling (Burke & Newton, 1983), but they are still met with opposition, especially from the old-school European experts (Ennis, 1983).

The best approach to this debate is to have the competitive cyclist try some form of strength work and see what the results actually will be. This was done by George Mount, U.S. professional who placed sixth in the 1976 Olympic road race. Mount experienced positive results, especially by gaining strength in those areas that cycling does not normally stress, that is, arms, shoulders, and upper back (Vernal, 1976). In fact, one of the real advantages to strength training is getting the body to its optimal level of strength in all parts, not just the obvious muscles such as quadriceps. Actual advantages to progressive-resistance training include:

1. Added strength
2. Muscular endurance
3. Prevention of injury
4. Rehabilitation of injury

Hardly a sport exists that cannot benefit from increased strength, and cycling is no exception. Most arguments against the use of weights will center around the old wives' tale about becoming muscle bound. Understandably a cyclist does not want to develop useless muscles, such as an 18-in. upper arm, that will only add to the body weight needed to pedal up a hill or toward a finish line. However, to actually increase the strength of a 13-in. arm by 20% to 50%, but not increase muscular bulk, will actually help the rider climb and/or sprint more effectively.

Actual muscle hypertrophy, or growth, is due to specific training and dietary regimens designed for that specific purpose. If the cyclist concentrates on strengthening muscles for cycling, rather than becoming a bodybuilder, no problems will occur. Certainly the amount of muscle tissue that will be developed is also a function of heredity. An occasional string-bean sprinter or "Incredible Hulk" road rider will surface, but generally certain body types will seek certain riding events because of the immediate differences in their initial success.

Program Planning

The real emphasis should be given to proper program planning. As with most sports these days, training should be cyclical in nature; that is, some specific differences in the training program should exist due to *periodization* (Stone, O'Brien, Garhammer, McMullan, & Rozenek, 1982). This term refers to the actual manipulation of training conditions in order to (a) achieve maximum strength results, (b) allow for proper peaking of the athlete's main sport, specifically cycling, and (c) provide variety in order to avoid physical and mental burnout.

The coach and rider must remember that the purpose of this training is to become a better cyclist, not a weight lifter. For example, during that part of the season when the rider is peaking for a best performance on the bike, he or she should not be concerned with achieving a personal record in the squat. Conversely, during the winter months, when activity with weights should be maximized, athletes should not be concerned with 400-mi weeks or improving their sprints.

The various parts of the training cycle are shown in Table 1. Ironically, these can be applied both to strength training and to cycling; only the language needs to be changed. The *transitional phase* helps the rider reduce time on the bike while adjusting the body to a new and different type of stress. This work is done in a simple fashion, with a minimum of equipment. Body weight resistance can be used for various exercises, thus avoiding the common problem of using too much weight too soon. Actual workout time should be short, with 1 to 3 sets of each exercise being done, consisting of 15 to 20 repetitions. The training can be done 2 to 3 times per week, allowing a gradual taper in road miles and letting the body get adequate rest.

After the muscles have been properly prepared, the *hypertrophy phase* begins, and the concentration is now on using a slightly heavier

Table 1   Seasonal Cycling and Weight Program

Weight Training Program	Road Rider	Track Rider (Sprint/Kilometer)
End season	September	September
Transitional	October (2 to 4 weeks)	October (4 weeks)
Hypertrophy	Nov.-Dec. (4 to 6 weeks)	Nov.-Dec. (4 to 6 weeks)
Basic strength	Dec.-Jan. (4 to 6 weeks)	Jan.-Feb. (8 weeks)
Power/in season	Jan.-Feb. (4 to 6 weeks)	March and April (8 weeks)
Maintenance	March into season	May-June: Depends on race schedule. Small cycles continue throughout year.

resistance while decreasing the number of repetitions. As the name implies, this phase is geared toward allowing the muscles to grow. This does not mean that body weight will increase; in fact, body composition may actually change, while body weight remains fairly constant. By working the muscles more intensely and allowing some growth, the body will be properly prepared for the next phase.

The *basic-strength phase* is geared toward increasing the actual strength potential of individual muscle groups and in using these separate groups in a coordinated effort. Resistance increases as repetitions are decreased. Actual exercises may also change during this time in order to test the ability of the body to move effectively in a unified effort and to allow for variation in training. To actually increase the rider's strength quickly is quite easy, but the real benefit to most riders will come from the conversion of this strength to power.

Power is the ability to use force in an explosive fashion. Increased power will allow the sprinter to jump more quickly, the road rider to bridge gaps faster, and to be able to do this in a repeated fashion, if necessary. The track rider wants this phase to occur just prior to the peak of the season. As a result, in the *power phase*, actual resistance is reduced, perhaps along with a reduction in the number of strength-training sessions each week, thus allowing for increased quality and quantity of training on the bike. Exercises are all done in an explosive manner, using timing devices where appropriate.

As this phase ends, the decision needs to be made as to how much, if any, maintenance training will be done. Because the rider will now be racing on a regular basis, the amount, duration, and intensity of strength work will be reduced. Continuing to train those weak points not normally stressed on the bike is frequently a good idea. This can be done with simple exercises, using circuits or body weight resistance exercises. This additional work allows the cyclist to maintain much of his or her new-found strength and also reduces the amount of strength

Table 2 Strength Training Program Phases

Phase	Purpose	Sets/Reps	Exercises	Intensity	Days/Week
Transitional	Adjust to strength training	1 to 3/15 to 20	General in nature: circuits, body weight resistance, etc.	Minimum	2 to 3
Hypertrophy	Build muscle tissue	3 to 4/8 to 12	4 to 6, specific muscle groups: quad/ glutes, biceps, triceps, abdominals, back, deltoids, gastroc	Moderate	3
Basic strength	Gain strength	5 to 7/1 to 6	3 to 5, combined muscle groups: concentrate on weak areas	Heavy (80% to 100%)	3
Power	Explosive power	5 to 6/1 to 15	3 to 4, specific muscle groups for cycling: partial squats, lunges, rowing	Moderate	2 to 3
Maintenance	Maintain strength	1 to 3/6 to 10	Work on 1 to 3 weak areas not directly strengthened while riding	Light	1 to 2

lost so that the next transitional phase is begun at a level of strength higher than the previous year. Table 2 shows how the phases and their components can be applied to the yearly plan of a cyclist's training.

Machine Versus Free Weights

Accompanying the argument over whether or not to train is the question of what is the best form of training—machines or free weights. Numerous claims by machine manufacturers are geared toward convincing the trainee that a particular line of apparatus will be superior to any other. Actually *any* training is better than none at all. If one or the other is more readily available to the athlete, or a preference exists toward one or the other, go with what feels best. As with bicycle components, a need exists to advertise and sell products. Seldom does anyone try to sell the public on the value of free weights, although the merits have been discussed in the literature.

Beyond the claims by machine manufacturers, machines give a feeling of comfort and safety. Free weights, on the other hand, are readily available without the cyclist's having to join a facility outfitted with a certain line of machines. During the cyclist's many days, weeks, or months on the road, it is convenient to store a barbell in the team van for use between races. More appropriately, free weights allow the body to exercise while having to maintain balance, a trait important to the cyclist. Machines usually allow the user to sit or lie down and exercise in only the specific direction or plane established by their structure. Also, more specific exercises for individual sports can be carried out with free weights.

Specific Versus Nonspecific Exercises

In order to get the best transfer to another sport, the strengthening exercises should be done in as close a pattern to the actual sport as possible. The most specific form of strength work for the cyclist would probably come from the ergometer (stationary bicycle). This, however, would not allow for the strengthening of muscle groups that are important to cycling but are not stressed by this activity. Generally, the hypertrophy stage is nonspecific; that is, the exercises need not closely resemble the activity of cycling. Individual muscle groups are being developed for later strength work. Again, most machines are suited for this type of training. Strength-phase training can be carried out in either a specific or nonspecific format. Some specific exercises may allow the body to get into a dangerous position, that is, back not flat or feet not evenly spaced below the athlete.

The best use of specific exercises is in the power and/or maintenance phases. Here the weights are lighter and speed of movement is most important. The author noticed several years ago some unique exercises being done by the U.S. Cycling Team at the Olympic Training Center in Colorado Springs, but the execution of the exercises left much to be desired. For example, the athletes were told to use "a maximum weight and to move at maximum speed." In order to train for speed, one would normally use a resistance in the 75% to 85% range, knowing that anything heavier would slow the movement. Doing squats or high pulls at a rapid pace will give better transfer, as the following conclusions indicate:

1. Low-power (low-speed, high-load) exercise produces greater increases in muscular force only at slow speeds.
2. High-power (high-speed, low-load) exercise produces increases in muscular force at all speeds of contraction at and below the training speed.
3. High-power exercise increases muscular endurance at high speeds more than low-power exercise increases muscular endurance at slow speeds.

Although the cyclists observed at the training center eventually squatted maximum weights, they could not do so at a maximum speed, nor could they maintain their positions to ensure a low incidence of injury.

Strength Training Exercises

An example of how the various phases can change during a cycle of strength training is shown in Table 3. These are only examples of exercises to be used and not a program that needs to be strictly followed. To prepare the lower back musculature, for example, one would begin the transitional phase with hyperextension, thereby isolating the muscles, but not using any large resistance. During the hypertrophy phase, stiff-legged deadlifts or good-morning exercises could be employed. Once the muscles have been properly prepared, power cleans or high pulls would be used in the basic-strength phase and power phase. For maintenance, hyperextension would again be employed, if necessary. Some imagination can be used to produce exercises of

2525 Training for Cycling 27

Table 3 Suggested Strength Training Exercises per Phase

Transitional	Hypertrophy	Basic Strength	Power	In Season
Day 1				
Trunk Curl	Squats	Push Press	Power Clean	Hyperextension
Dips	Pullover (straight arm)	Power Clean	Dips	Trunk Curl
Leg Extension/Leg Curl	Trunk Curl	Squats	Partial Squat	Squats
Pull-Ups	Calf Raise	Trunk Curl	Trunk Curl	Dips
Hyperextension	Dips	Calf Raise	Bent-Over Rowing	Pull-Ups
or	Hyperextension			
General Circuit	Pull-Ups			
Day 2				
Twist/Side Bend	Dumbbell Press	Bench Press	High Pulls	Partial Squats
Leg Press	Hanging Leg Raise	High Pulls	Push Press	Dips
Lat Pulldown	Good Morning	Barbell Twist (1 end weight)	Squats	Pull-Ups
Hanging Leg Raise	Leg Press	Partial Squats	Trunk Curl	Calf Raise
Press	Trunk Curl			
or	Bent-Over Rowing			
General Circuit				
Day 3				
Trunk Curl	Squats	Power Clean	Power Clean	
Lunges	Pullover (bent arm)	Speed Squat	Pull-Ups	
Calf Raise (single leg)	Trunk Curl	Incline Press	Partial Squats	
Hyperextension	Still-Legged Deadlift	Rowing	Trunk Curl	
Upright Rowing	Pull-Ups			
or	Calf Raise			
General Circuit	Dips			

a specific nature. It is beyond the scope of this chapter to outline every movement that could be of use. Rather, some basic exercises are listed, along with figures showing key positions. It is always a good idea to recruit the advice of a knowledgeable strength instructor.

The popularity of strength training, along with the lack of organized certification, can frustrate the cyclist by exposing him or her to many so-called experts whose advice may be 180° different. The bodybuilder type of coach may try to convince the rider to stay in a hypertrophy type of training, while the powerlifter may expect the cyclist to perform a squat in a similar fashion to a competitive movement, thereby exposing the rider to too intense a load supported by a poorly prepared musculature and dependent on excessive belts, wraps, and suits to lift maximum weights. The weightlifter might have the cyclist concentrate mainly on power cleans and snatches. The machine enthusiast might have the rider do only slow, nonspecific movements. The bottom line is that all these opinions have merit, but the cyclist must learn to think for himself or herself.

The following exercises are common strength-training exercises used by cyclists:

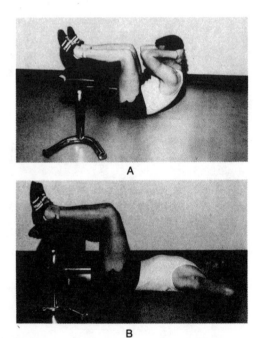

A

B

Figure 1   Trunk Curl

The feet can be flat or crossed above the body or on a bench. By avoiding a stationary position of the feet, the thigh and hip muscles are not used, only the abdominal muscles. Slowly contract the abdominal muscles, placing the chin on the chest and attempt to touch the elbows to knees. The actual movement is only about 6 to 8 in.

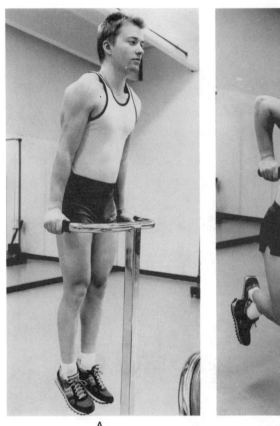
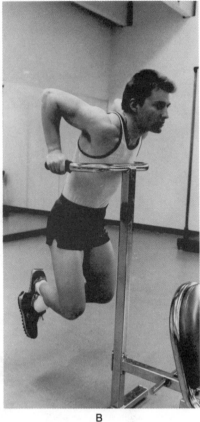

A   B

Figure 2 Dips

From a fully extended arm position, lower the body by bending the elbows. After lowering the body as far as possible, push upward to locked arm position. If the rider is too weak to push back to the completed position, only the negative (eccentric) portion should be done. Take about 6 s to lower the body, resisting all the way. Use a bench or chair to hop back to Position A and repeat. After several weeks of doing the movement in this manner, the rider should be strong enough to do the movement in the normal fashion. This technique can be used for pull-ups also.

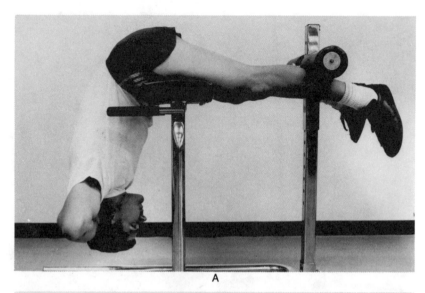

A

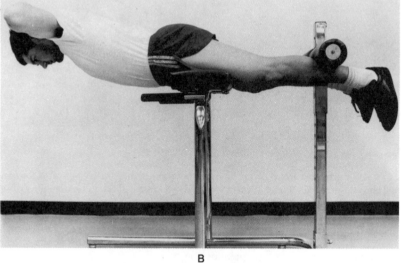

B

Figure 3   Hyperextension

Although a padded apparatus is preferred, this exercise can be done off the edge of a table or chair if necessary. From Position A, slowly contract the lower back muscles until the trunk is parallel to the ground. There is no great need to rise higher than Position B. The movement can be done with the back flat throughout or with the back initially rounded, finishing with the back flat. Additional weight may be held behind the neck as the rider becomes stronger.

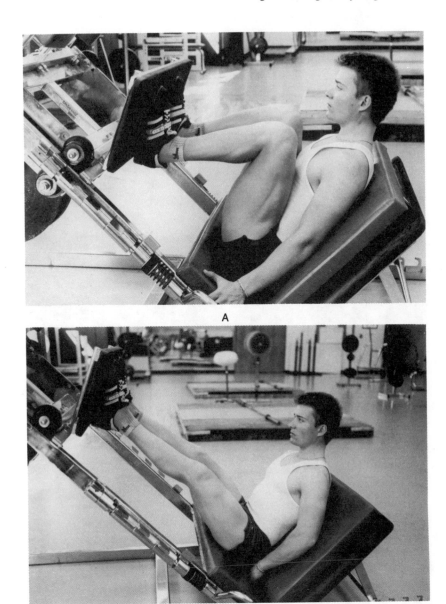

A

B

Figure 4 Leg Press

Various leg-press machines are available (horizontal, vertical, or slant, as pictured).
Regardless of the machine, knees are bent to the desired level and then returned to a
locked position.

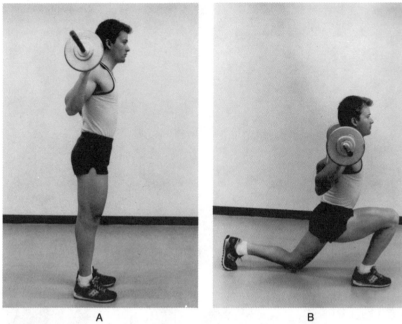

A   B

Figure 5   Lunge

Start with the bar on the trapezius (upper back) muscles (Position A). Step forward and sink down to the desired Position B. Push up and back to A. Repeat with the other leg. Very little weight is needed. The depth of movement can be adjusted to specific knee flexion as in cycling.

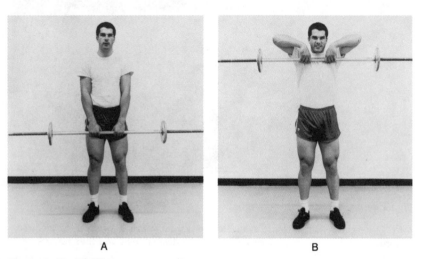

A   B

Figure 6   Upright Row

Using a shoulder-width or slightly more narrow grip, assume Position A. Using the trapezius, arm, and deltoid muscles, raise the weight to about sternum level. Elbows should raise up to the top of the head. Lower slowly and repeat.

A

B

C

D

Figure 7   Squats

The real base for any program, squats can be done throughout the training cycle, simply adjusting the depth, intensity, or speed. A shows the position for normal squatting, with the bar on the trapezius and shoulders. (A towel or pad can be used if necessary.) Feet are about hip width and generally toes are pointed slightly outward or straight ahead. It is most important to keep the back flat and not let it round. The bar should remain over the feet throughout the movement. Slowly bend the knees until the proper depth is found.

Popular myths from 20 years ago have kept people from doing full squats. Assuming proper style is used, squats are no more dangerous than any other exercise. The descent should be done under control, taking 1 to 3 s to complete the lowering phase. Be sure not to bounce on recovery. It is beyond the scope of this chapter to explain everything about squatting, but be prepared to hear many different opinions.

The full squat (D) can be used during the hypertrophy phase, because the weight is light and repetitions moderate. As weight increases, the depth can be adjusted so that the tops of the thighs become parallel to the floor and then the athlete starts up (C). The partial (B) or 1/2 squat can be used during any phase, but most positively during the basic-strength phase. Large amounts of weight can be employed. It is important to have a strong trunk in the case of heavy weights. Abdominal and lower-back strength are important in order to maintain position.

Speed squats are used during the power phase. The athlete descends normally but then rises as quickly as possible. A coach or assistant uses a stopwatch to time the ascent. The watch is started as soon as upward movement is detected and stopped when the knees fully straighten out. Rather than compete against another rider, the athlete should strive to improve his or her own time at a particular weight. Keeping each squat under 1 s, at 80% to 85% of max, for example, will help in the recruitment of fast-twitch fibers. Less time may be a goal with lighter weights. Keep a cumulative total of repetitions.

A

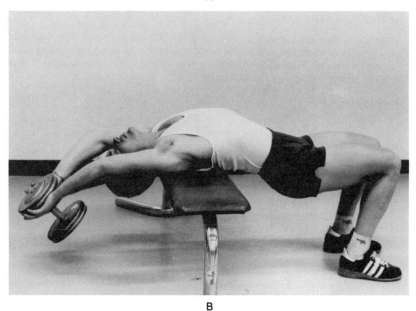

B

Figure 8   Straight-Arm Pullover

Use light weight (15 to 25 lb barbell or dumbbell). Start as in Position A and inhale deeply while lowering the weight to Position B. Exhale as the weight is returned to starting position. This is used to regain breath after high-repetition squats. The weight is *not* important. It is a breathing exercise.

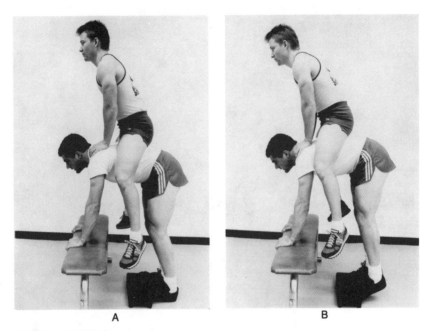

A   B

Figure 9   Calf Raise

A special machine may be used or a barbell across the shoulders or a dumbbell in one
hand (one leg at a time) or a partner as in the figures of what is called "donkey raise."
The use of a board under the toes helps to add stretch to the calf muscles (A). Keep
the knee straight. Use high repetitions (15 to 30).

C

Figure 10 Good Morning

The name came from a gentleman's motion of bowing at the waist while saying "good morning" to the ladies. Start with the bar on the back (A) and flex the knees slightly, while bending forward. The lower back may be rounded (B) or flat (C). Use light-to-moderate weights only, as the position can be stressful if too much resistance is offered. One repetition is completed by returning to the starting position.

A   B

Figure 11   Bent-Over Rowing

Knees slightly flexed, back mostly flat (A), the weight is drawn up to the chest or abdominal area (B) with the arms, shoulders, and latissimus muscles of the back. Do not
allow the weight to drop when returning to the starting position. The U.S. Cycling Team
does this exercise leaning the chest against an incline bench and using two dumbbells.

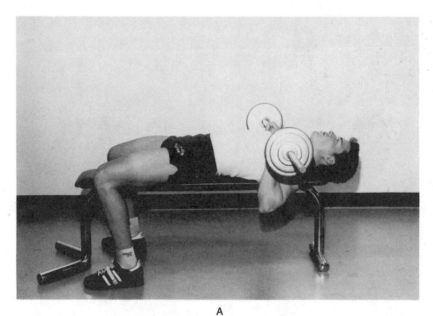

A

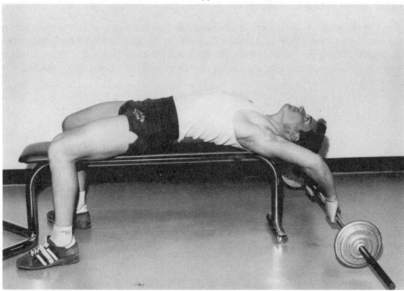

B

Figure 12   Bent-Arm Pullover

Much more weight can be used in the straight-arm version. Weight is placed on the chest (A) and then passed close by the face until it rests on or near the ground (B). A large inhalation occurs during this phase. When returning the weight to the chest, exhale completely.

A   B

Figure 13   Stiff-Legged Deadlift

Keeping the knees slightly bent is advisable, despite the name of the exercise. From the starting position (A), round the back and lower the weight until it has gone as low as desired. Doing this exercise from the floor will limit the range of motion, whereas doing it on a bench will give maximum stretch to back and hamstring muscles.

Figure 14 Push Press

Actually a "cheat press," the legs are used to start the bar's movement but triceps and deltoids finish the lockout phase. Hold the bar as in A, letting the bar rest on the frontal deltoids, not just the bent arms. Bend the knees a few inches (B), then combine leg and arm thrust to get the bar over the head (C). This includes rising on the toes. The lockout is completed (D) with feet flat on the floor again. Do not bend backward. Return to A while bending the knees. Begin again.

Figure 15   Power Clean

An excellent combined muscle movement for the strength or power phases. Start with feet flat (A), knees over toes, feet about hip width apart. Use the legs and hips to raise the bar to Position B. Note the arms are still straight and the back flat. After the bar passes the knees, the ankles and knees will bend as in C, placing the bar on the thighs. A forceful jump will result in the bar moving quickly upward (D). A slight dip in the knees will afix the bar on the shoulders (E). This exercise uses the bigger muscles of the body and helps to develop a quick, explosive movement. The pull and placement on the shoulders will take about 1 s to execute.

Figure 16 High Pulls

Heavier weights can be used because the bar is only being pulled up (D), rather than actually "cleaned" to the shoulders. All the other positions remain identical to the power clean. Be sure the back is flat and the hips do not lift too quickly.

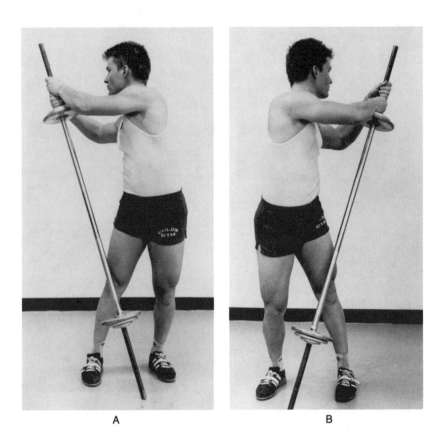

A   B

Figure 17   Barbell Twist

In order to exercise the muscles used in rotational activity, some form of this exercise should be employed. The oblique muscles of the abdominal wall will help to rotate the body and weight from A to B and back. Do not depend on arm muscles. Be sure to keep hips stable.

A　　　　　　　　　　　　B

Figure 18　Heavy Partial Squats

These can be done from a position as in A where the bar is resting on pins in a power rack. Keep feet flat and back flat. Rise as quickly as possible. All cyclists should be able to work up to the range of 300 to 800 lb in this position.

The actual exercises are not as important as getting good representation of all major muscle groups (legs, abdominals, back, arms, shoulders, etc.). Feel free to use other exercises or variations of those described. Remember to modify workouts as various phases change.

General Notes for the Cyclist

Each strength-training session must begin and end with some stretching movements. This serves the purpose of warming up and down and also of increasing the specific flexibility of different muscle groups. Racers spend so much time in the same position that their flexibility is frequently impaired. The emphasis on increasing flexibility will lead to better riding, fewer injuries, and increased range of motion for weight-lifting exercises.

Aside from stretching, it is a good idea to ride rollers, an ergometer, or an actual bicycle as an additional warm-down after weights. This short period of time (5 to 10 min) will help the cyclist to loosen his or her muscles in a familiar pattern. To become stronger at the end of the strength-training cycle is pointless if the rider has lost smoothness on the bike.

Safety should be a key factor. If injured while lifting weights, the rider will be kept away from weights during recuperation and may perform less well on the bike. Use of spotters on certain free-weight exercises can be extremely important. Self-discipline is extremely important in the weight room.

Dressing warmly will help prevent injuries, especially during the cold months. A weight-lifting belt may provide a feeling of security but is not absolutely necessary. Attention should be paid to proper shoes, particularly when heavy loads are placed on the upper torso or are overhead. The sole should not compress excessively, nor should the heel design lead to any instability or loss of balance.

Strength training can be fun and should definitely lead to better performance on the cycle. While many top road riders may not do weight training, particularly the European professionals, this does not mean it is not useful. If the typical U.S. amateur raced as much as the European pro, he or she would not have time for weights and would most probably be stronger because of the increased cycling. For the road cyclist, the ultimate strength development will still come on the cycle, particularly in the form of hill climbs, intervals, and road sprints. For the track cyclist, weight training can be the quickest way to develop added strength and power.

References

Burke, E., & Newton, H. (1983). Improved cycling performance through strength training. *National Strength and Conditioning Association Journal, 5*(3), 6-7, 70-71.

Ennis, P. (1983). The doctor in cycling. *Cycling U.S.A., 6*(6), 8-9.

Stone, M., O'Brien, H., Garhammer, J., McMullan, J., & Rozenek, R. (1982). A theoretical model of strength training. *National Strength and Conditioning Association Journal, 4*(4), 36-39.

Vernal, P. (1976). 'Smilin' George Mount. *Bike World, 5*(12), 30-32.

CHAPTER 3

Flexibility Standards
of the U.S. Cycling Team

Mitchell L. Feingold, DPM
Consultant for the U.S. Cycling Team
Podiatrist in private practice in San Diego, CA

Good physical performance is based on strength, endurance, speed, coordination, and flexibility. In the past, flexibility has been the area that has received the least amount of attention from the U.S. Cycling Team. In 1983 I initiated a team flexibility program that covers an understanding of flexibility, the reasons for it, the measurable criteria of flexibility, and a concept of therapeutic stretching to achieve these criteria.

Flexibility

Simply defined, flexibility is the ability of a joint to move through its normal range of motion. The structures that can limit this range of motion are (a) the bony architecture of the joint, (b) the ligaments around the joint, (c) the fibrous joint capsule, and (d) the tendons and muscles that cross the joint. The most common cause of decreased flexibility is muscle contracture, or muscle tightness. Fortunately, of the four limiting factors, muscle contracture is the one we can do the most about.

The importance of having an unrestricted, normal range of motion at each joint level in the body cannot be overemphasized. Clinical experience has shown that a significant decrease in flexibility is associated with an increase in stress-related injuries. The human body functions as a unit, and each joint must go through a specific range of motion for the body, as a whole, to accomplish its task. A decreased range of motion in one joint requires compensation in other joints to take up the slack. In other words, if one area of the body lacks sufficient range of motion, other areas of the body will be forced to increase their relative motion and experience increased stress.

Another factor is that muscles work in groups. For example, the hamstrings, which cause the knee to bend or flex, work against the quadriceps, which cause the knee to straighten out or extend. If the hamstrings are tight, the quadriceps will have to exert more force in straightening the knee to overcome the tight hamstrings. Sudden stretches made on tight muscles in performing an athletic activity can also lead to muscle strains and tears.

By having a normal range of motion at each joint level, the body thus tends to become more efficient as demonstrated by smoothness of motion and decreased fatigue. The chance of stress-related injuries decreases. This translates into long-term, more effective training, which can lead to improved performance.

Flexibility Program

A good flexibility program should have specific criteria that the cyclist can measure and duplicate so that he or she can identify specific flexibility problems. Individuals will vary from one another in their flexibility levels and the ease with which they can achieve the criteria.

The important principle in determining flexibility is to *isolate* each joint and muscle group that is being tested. This is done in such a way that the inflexibility of one joint is not masked by an overly flexible adjacent joint. An example of this is bending down to touch the toes while keeping the knees straight to demonstrate hamstring flexibility. It is not uncommon to be able to palm the floor, but when the hamstrings are isolated the cyclist is not able to meet the criteria of hamstring flexibility. The cyclist is able to palm the floor because of an overly lax lower back, which is able to mask the fact that the hamstrings are tight. Due to the physiology of the muscle-stretch responses, the individual must be relaxed while each muscle group is tested passively. This will give a passive muscle length that is the best condition for duplicating testing.

The basic standards of flexibility that are being used can easily be reproduced and achieved. Clinical experience has shown that athletes meeting these standards suffer less from stress-related injuries. The athletes state that their performance is smoother and more efficient. Although at this point no concrete research data exists to back up the numbers that are being used, there must be a point from which to start in setting standards. Therefore, what follows is the result of the accumulated data currently in the physical therapy, physical medicine, and sports medicine literature along with the combined clinical experience of those practitioners applying the standards.

When testing the range of motion, practitioners are concerned with what is considered a free range of motion; that is, the part will move freely with no resistance. The point at which resistance is first felt marks the end of the range of motion in that direction.

A Flexibility Exam

The following tests measure the flexibility of the major muscle groups.

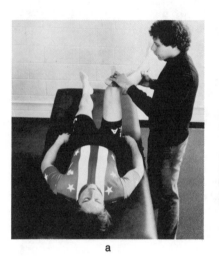 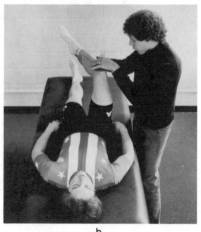

a   b

Figure 1   Hip Rotation

The starting position is lying on your back (supine) with both legs extended straight out and together. The hip that is being tested is bent 90° so that the thigh is straight up and the knee is bent 90°. From this position the examiner should easily be able to rotate the leg in an arc a total of 90°. By moving the leg toward the examiner (see Figure 1a), the hip joint is being rotated internally. There should be a minimum of 30° of internal rotation at the hip. As the leg is moved away from the examiner (see Figure 1b) across the midline of your body, the hip is being externally rotated. It does not matter whether it is 30° and 60° or 50° and 40°, as long as there is a total of 90° rotation.

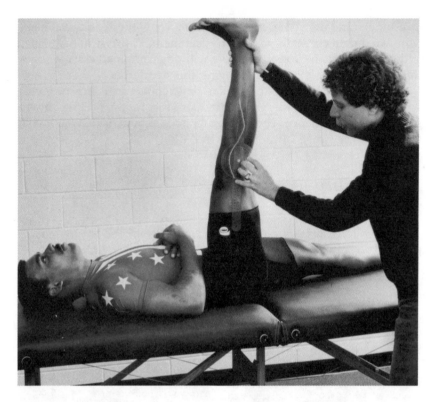

Figure 2   Hamstrings

Lying on your back in the same starting position as for the hip-rotation exam, you should be able to extend the leg that is bent at 90° all the way to 180° (straight up) with the foot bent 90° at the ankle (see Figure 2). Make sure that the leg not being tested is lying extended straight on the table and is not bent at the knee in an attempt to compensate for a tight hamstring.

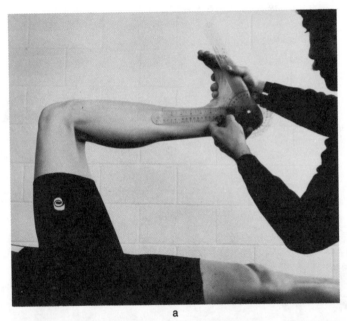

a

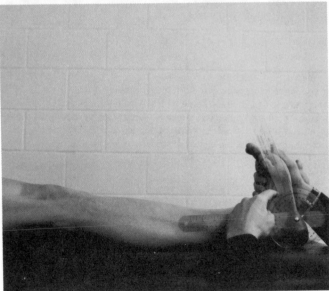

b

Figure 3   Ankle Joint

Lying on your back with the knee flexed, you should be able to bend the foot 20° toward the leg from a right angle (see Figure 3a). This will test the tightness of the soleus muscle, which is one of the two major muscles of the calf. Lying on your back with the knee fully extended, again the foot is flexed 20° on the leg at the ankle joint (see Figure 3b). This measures the tightness of the gastrocnemius muscle.

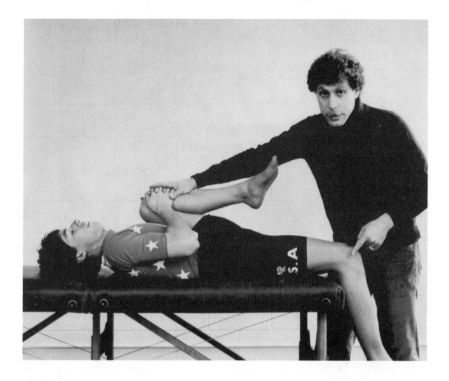

Figure 4 Iliopsoas Test

This test measures the tightness of the iliopsoas muscle group in front of the hip. For this test you lie on your back with both knees extending over the edge of the table as shown in Figure 4. To test the left side, you should be able to grab the knee of the right leg with both hands and pull it to your chest (keep your head back on the table). If the iliopsoas muscle on the left side is not tight, the left thigh will remain on the table with the knee bent at 90°. If the leg begins to straighten, or the thigh raises up off the table, tightness of this muscle group is indicated.

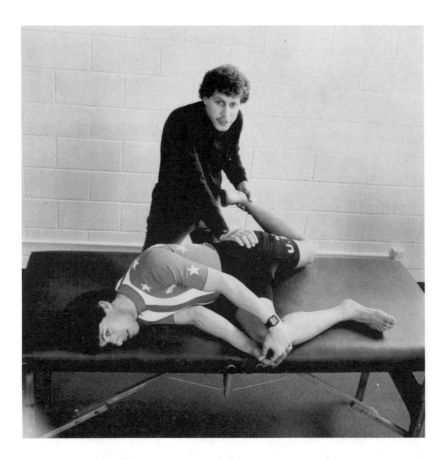

Figure 5 I.T.B. Test

This test measures the tightness of the iliotibial band on the lateral (outside) aspect of the thigh. For this test you lie on one side with the leg being tested on top as shown in Figure 5. The hip and knee of the bottom leg are flexed while grasping the knee with both hands. The examiner stands behind you and steadies the pelvis with one hand, while grasping the ankle of the top leg with the other hand. The examiner then bends the top knee 90° and the entire leg is pulled backward. The knee should drop below the horizontal plane at least 15°. If it does not, this indicates tightness of the iliotibial band.

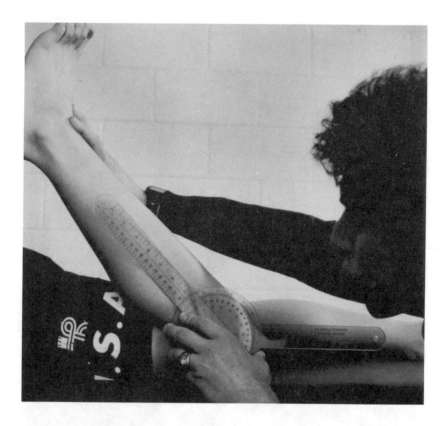

Figure 6   Quadriceps Test

This tests the tightness of the rectus femoris muscle in front of the thigh. For this test you lie on your stomach (prone). The examiner uses 2 fingers placed in front of the ankle of the leg being tested and bends the leg backward until it meets resistance (see Figure 6). You should be able to touch the heel of the leg being tested to the gluteal (butt) muscles. An angle of at least 135° should be formed between the leg and the table. Make sure that the pelvis is not rotated in an attempt to compensate and lift the gluteal muscles.

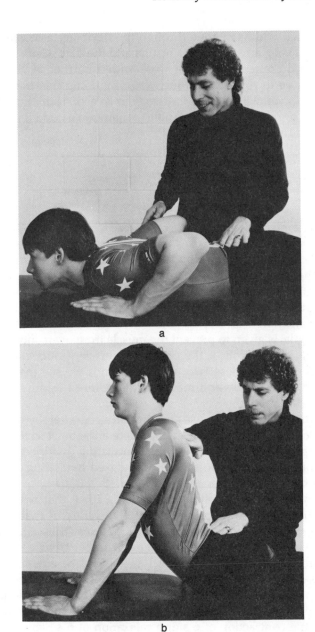

Figure 7   Spine Extension

This test is used to measure the tightness of the muscles in front of the spinal column. Lying on your stomach with the hands and shoulders positioned as though you were to do a push-up, you then straighten your arms while arching your back and keeping the pelvis on the table (see Figure 7a). You should be able to bring your shoulders into a vertical position with the elbows extended and the pelvis remaining on the table as shown in Figure 7b.

Now that you have gone through the flexibility assessment test, you should keep a record of the results and the date. Once you know how to do these tests, and you work with a partner, it should take only a minute to run through the exam. By doing this exam at least once a week, you will be able to assess your level of flexibility and know where you are tight. You will be able to maintain a good level of flexibility throughout your training.

Therapeutic Stretching Exercises

When a muscle is stretched, a reflex reaction takes place in the muscle. A signal is sent that causes the muscle to contract in an attempt to prevent overstretching. This is how the body protects itself from injury. The force of the contraction is related to the force of the stretch. If the stretch is hard and jerky, then the stretch-reflex contraction will be proportional to that force. If the stretch is easy and slow, the stretch-reflex contraction will be easy and slow. When a muscle contracts, another signal is given to prevent the muscle from overcontracting and to stop the contraction of the opposing muscle group that is being stretched. Keeping these two points in mind, we see that a stretch should be done slowly and mildly to the point of tightness and not pain and discomfort.

Another principle is to use an active stretch, whereby one muscle group is contracted to stretch the opposite antagonist muscle group. An example of this is the use of the contracting quadriceps muscles in the front of the thigh to stretch the relaxed hamstring muscles in the back of the thigh.

When a muscle is contracted against a force that will not let it shorten (isometric contraction), the stretch reflex of that muscle is momentarily inhibited when the muscle relaxes, thus allowing that muscle to be stretched further. The muscle to be stretched should be isolated to make sure that the stretch is going to be effective with no compensatory movements from other parts of the body. Stretching, if done properly, is safe and effective. It should never be done to the point of pain. Each stretch should be held for 15 s followed by either an isometric contraction of 6 s or a relaxation of 6 s. This should be repeated 3 times per stretch, always finishing with a stretch.

For a stretching program to be effective it should be done a minimum of 4 times a week, preferably every day of the week. Allow 20 to 30 min for each session. The stretches should be done within 2 hours prior to cycling. After a hard workout, a good idea is to stretch to help prevent muscle soreness the day following the ride. There should be a warm-up period at the beginning of the ride and a cool-down period at the end of the ride.

The specific stretches that follow are therapeutic stretches used to meet a specific criteria of flexibility. They should not be confused with warm-up stretches and other types of stretches used in yoga and dance. Clinical experience has shown that people who attempt to do the stretches used in dance and yoga, and are not able to meet the basic criteria of flexibility, tend to develop injuries in attempting the other stretches. First achieve the basic level of flexibility through therapeutic stretching exercises before embarking on other stretching programs. The goal is to achieve and maintain flexibility. This will be accomplished only by making the flexibility evaluation and exercises a routine part of your training program. Maintaining flexibility during the off season is especially important. This will help maintain good all-around fitness so that your body will be ready for training. I coined a slogan that seems to apply to all athletes: "To perform well, and be consistent, an athlete must maintain good *musculoskeletal hygiene.*"

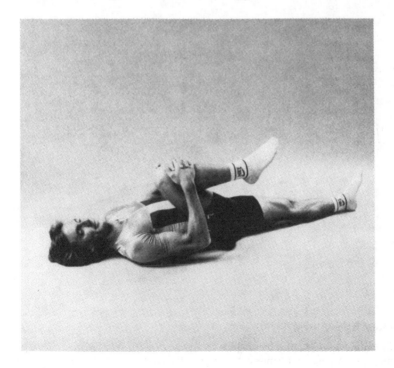

Figure 8   Upper-Hamstring Stretch

Lying on your back, bend the knee of the leg you are going to stretch and pull it to your chest (see Figure 8). Make sure the opposite leg is straight and not bent at the knee. Hold the stretch for 15 s, relax for 6 s, and repeat 2 more times. Repeat with the other leg.

a

b

Figure 9   Hamstring Stretch

Lying on your back, flex the thigh 90° and the knee 90° (see Figure 9a). Stabilize the thigh by clasping your hands behind it near the knee. Now bring your leg straight up with the foot bent at 90° (as shown in Figure 9b). Hold for 15 s, then do an isometric contraction of the hamstring. This is done by trying to bring the thigh down to the floor but keeping it from moving. Repeat 3 times and then stretch the opposite leg.

Figure 10   Hamstring Buddy Stretch

While lying on your back, have your partner grasp the leg and attempt to bring it straight up (see Figure 10). Hold the leg in that position for 15 s and then try to bring your leg down while your partner resists the motion for 6 s. Finally relax your leg while your partner attempts again to bring it to the upright position. Repeat 3 times. Make sure that your partner straightens the leg to the point of tightness and not pain. You will know when flexibility has been achieved when the leg can easily be brought to the upright position. Do not attempt to go beyond this position. Stretch the opposite leg.

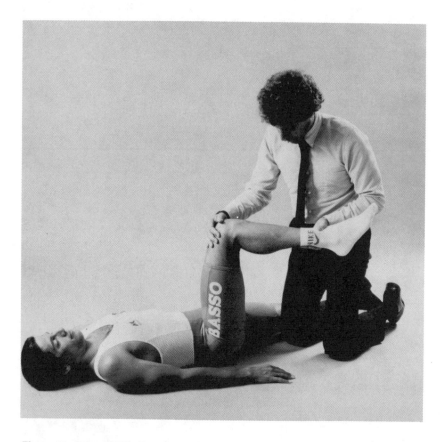

Figure 11   Internal Hip Rotation

While lying on your back, flex the thigh and the knee 90°. Your partner should stabilize the thigh by grasping it near the knee with one hand and stabilize the leg by grasping the foot with the other hand (see Figure 11). While maintaining the thigh and knee at 90°, your partner should then rotate the leg away from the opposite leg. Be sure to tell your partner to stop at the moment you feel tightness in the hip. Have your partner hold the leg in this position for 15 s and then attempt an isometric contraction moving in the opposite direction for 6 s. Repeat this 3 times and then rotate the opposite hip.

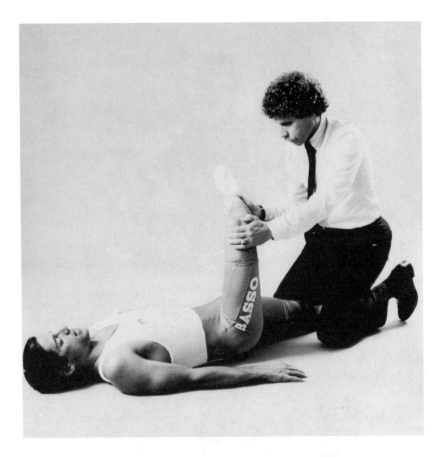

Figure 12   External Hip Rotation

The positioning for external hip rotation is the same as for the internal hip rotation. In this stretch your partner will move your foot across the midline of the body to rotate the hip externally (see Figure 12). Go to the point of tightness, hold 15 s, and then attempt an isometric contraction for 6 s. Repeat 3 times and then rotate the opposite hip.

a

b

Figure 13 Groin Muscles

While sitting on the floor, preferably with your back straight against the wall, bring the soles of your feet together (as shown in Figure 13a). Move your feet as close to the groin as possible. Attempt to bring the outside of your knees to the floor as shown in Figure 13b. Hold for 15 s. Next lock your hands together and place the elbows on the inside of the knees. Finally do an isometric contraction by trying to bring the knees together. Hold for 6 s. Repeat 3 times.

a

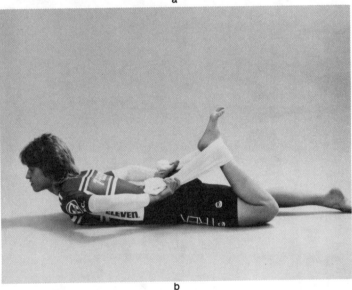

b

Figure 14 Quadriceps Stretch

While lying on your stomach, grab the ankle of the leg you are going to stretch (see Figure 14a). Attempt to bring the heel of the foot to the gluteal (butt) region. If you are able to do this, and feel no tightness in the quadriceps area, begin to raise the thigh off the floor until you do feel tightness. Hold for 15 s and relax for 6 s. Repeat 3 times. Make sure that you keep the knees together and that you are not rotating the pelvis while you are doing this stretch. If you are unable to grab the ankle because of quadricep tightness, wrap a towel around the ankle and pull via the towel as shown in Figure 14b. Repeat on the other side.

a

b

Figure 15   Low Back-Extension Stretch

Lying on your stomach with your hands and shoulders positioned as though you were to do a push-up, straighten your arms while arching your back, keeping your pelvis on the floor (see Figures 15a and b). You should attempt to bring your shoulders into a vertical position with the elbows straightened out and your pelvis remaining on the floor. Hold this for 15 s, relax for 6 s, and repeat 3 times.

Figure 16 Iliopsoas Stretch

Standing with one foot in front of the other, the feet approximately 2 to 3 ft apart, bend both knees and lift the heel of the rear foot off the floor (see Figure 16). Move your pelvis forward while bringing the thigh of the leg you are stretching behind the hip. The stretch should be felt on the upper part of the thigh and in front of the hip joint primarily. Hold for 15 s, relax for 6 s, and repeat 3 times. Repeat for the other side.

Figure 17   I.T.B. Stretch

To stretch the left iliotibial band, hold the wall for support with your left hand. Cross your right leg in front of the left and bring the outside of your right foot next to the outside of your left as shown in Figure 17. Making sure that you do not rotate your pelvis left or right or bend forward at the waist, lean into your left side, bringing your left hip closer to the wall that you are holding. You should feel a stretch on the outside of your left hip and upper thigh. Hold for 15 s, relax 6 s, and repeat 3 times. Reverse this procedure for the other leg.

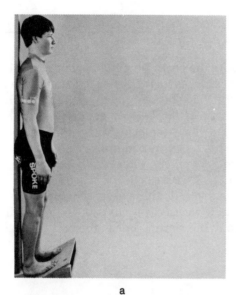

a

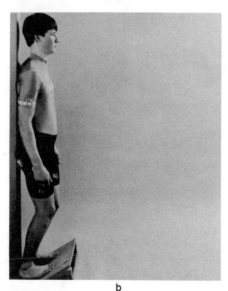

b

Figure 18   Calf Stretch

The ideal way to stretch the calf muscles is to use a wedge that makes a 30° angle with the floor as shown in Figure 18a. Place the low end of the wedge near the wall. Position your feet parallel to each other with the toes pointing toward the upper end of the wedge, while leaning your back against the wall. The closer the wedge is moved toward the wall the greater the stretch. Make sure your heels remain on the wedge surface. With the knees straightened, hold the position for 15 s. This will stretch the gastrocnemius muscles. Now bend the knees and hold the position for 15 s to stretch the soleus muscles (see Figure 18b). Repeat 3 times.

Summary

This concludes the basic set of therapeutic stretches for the cyclist. Although other stretches have been described by other authors, these particular stretches have been found to be the most effective in achieving the basic criteria of flexibility. Never stretch to the point of pain or discomfort. Do the stretches slowly and not abruptly. Stretch routinely. If you have a current injury, seek the advice of medical personnel. If you are extremely inflexible when you start this program, it will take from 2 to 4 weeks before you see significant improvement. You will improve if you do these exercises correctly and consistently. Good *musculoskeletal hygiene* is up to you. Good luck in your training, and may you go to the starting line in the best condition that you can be in.

CHAPTER 4

Effects of Saddle Height and Pedaling Cadence on Power Output and Efficiency

Robert J. Gregor
Stuart G. Rugg
University of California, Los Angeles

Power output is of prime importance to competitive cyclists. The relative power needed to move the bicycle under varied environmental conditions is something each rider must contend with on a daily basis. The ability to apply forces at the velocities required in training and competition is a major concern. Consequently, the correct choice of gear ratio, pedaling cadence, and position on the bike (i.e., saddle height) becomes critical to successful performance.

When discussing performance, two major issues arise. One concerns the efficiency of the rider and the other his or her power output. The concept of efficiency in competitive cycling has many elements. Questions related to the rider's efficiency, technique, and power-generating capabilities must be considered. Additional questions relate to the efficiency of the bicycle itself. Certainly it should be designed to capitalize on the rider's body structure and physiological capabilities to ensure an optimal performance. Considering the many variables involved, it is difficult, in reality, to separate the rider from the bike. Therefore, we must consider them as one integrated unit or performance will suffer.

Because efficiency is extensively discussed in the literature, this chapter will not focus on the many problems associated with its measurement. However, some comments are necessary regarding its definition and application to cycling. Physiological efficiency may be defined as the ratio of work accomplished to total energy expended (Gaesser & Brooks, 1975). Mechanical efficiency, discussed by Cavanagh in chapter 5, will be referred to as the rider's ability to effectively apply forces to the cranks. To the cyclist, the practical measure of work is the time taken to get from start to finish. The goal, therefore, is to match the mechanical efficiency of the bike to the physiological and mechanical efficiency of the rider to ensure the shortest possible time between start and finish at the lowest possible cost. For example, in short sprints the focus is on more mechanical issues because metabolism of long-term energy stores is not critical. However, in road races the proper use of long-term energy stores becomes critical and, while mechanical concerns are still important (effective application of forces and mechanical efficiency of the bike), attention must also be given to the physiology of the rider.

Human power output (pedaling cadence × load) has been well documented in the literature. The concern to the cyclist is not necessarily how much power he or she can produce, but rather how effectively his or her resources can be used to propel a bicycle. Because we are discussing power and efficiency as related to cadence and saddle height, we must keep in mind that these measures are not independent of one another. The many concerns of coaches and riders discussed in this book are closely interrelated. With this in mind, it is our objective to discuss saddle-height adjustments and cycling cadence in light of their effect on efficient transmission of power from the rider to the cycle.

Saddle-Height Adjustments

It is well known by competitive cyclists that (a) proper bicycle adjustments are essential for successful performance and (b) a change in one dimension cannot be made without affecting the other dimensions. For example, crank length cannot be changed without due consideration of saddle height and vice versa. Because adjustments of certain dimensions on the bicycle will affect the operating range of the leg muscles and consequently their force-production capabilities, one scientific investigation varied pedaling speed, work load, and frame characteristics (seat height) and sought an explanation for their results in the length-tension and force-velocity properties of skeletal muscle (Åstrand, 1953). Force production as well as the rate at which this tension can be developed is of concern to the cyclist. Specifically, changes in saddle height will alter the range of motion of the legs and subsequently the length changes experienced by the leg muscles. Pedaling cadence, then, would relate to the velocity of contraction and rate of force development in these same muscles. However, before we discuss these relationships in cycling, it would be useful to review these two fundamental properties of skeletal muscle.

Length-Tension Relationships

The total length-tension curve, as described for skeletal muscle fibers, "consists of a series of straight lines connected by short curved regions" (Aidley, 1978, p. 213). Although isometric tension is proportional to the number of interacting cross bridges (see Figures 1a and 1b), total tension, including passive connective tissue tension, increases as length increases (see Figure 1c). It would appear from the preceding discussion that, up to a certain level, increasing the initial length of the muscles of the lower limb might result in their increased ability to produce tension during the propulsive phase of cycling. In fact, early studies that varied saddle height reported that as muscle length increased, efficiency appeared to increase. This was attributed to the increased ability of the muscle to apply force in its elongated condition. Certain cycle modifications that increase the initial length of the muscle might, then, increase the cyclist's ability to exert tension.

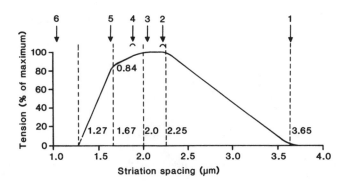

Figure 1(a) The isometric tension (active increment) of a frog muscle fiber, measured as a percentage of its maximum value, at different sarcomere lengths. The numbers 1 to 6 refer to the myofilament positions shown in Figure 1(b). From "The Variation in Isometric Tension With Sarcomere Length in Vertebrate Muscle Fibres" by A.M. Gordon, A.F. Huxley, & F.J. Julian, 1966, *Journal of Physiology*, **184**, pp. 170-192. Reprinted with permission.

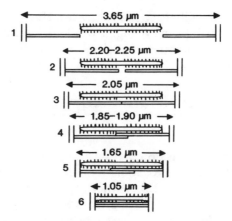

Figure 1(b) Myofilament arrangements at different lengths. The sarcomere lengths corresponding to the positions labeled 1 to 6 are indicated by the arrows in Figure 1(a). From "The Variation in Isometric Tension With Sarcomere Length in Vertebrate Muscle Fibres" by A.M. Gordon, A.F. Huxley, & F.J. Julian, 1966, *Journal of Physiology*, **184**, pp. 170-192. Reprinted with permission.

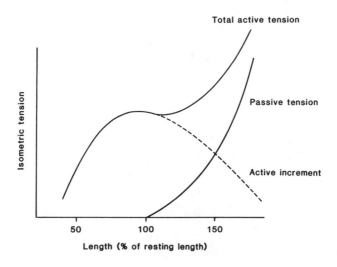

Figure 1(c) The length-tension relation of a muscle. From *The physiology of excitable cells* by D.J. Aidley, 1978, London: Cambridge University Press. Reprinted with permission.

Force-Velocity Relationships

The tension produced by the contractile component depends on the rate at which it is shortened as well as on its initial length (see Figure 2). From the force-velocity relationship detailed by Hill (1938), the ability of individual muscles to apply tension apparently decreases as the velocity of shortening increases. The reasons for this decline in tension development at higher rates of shortening become clear if one views the actions of the muscle at the fiber level. As the velocity of shortening increases, the chance of cross-bridge formation at any one site will decrease; the total number of cross bridges formed will decrease; and therefore the tension developed by the muscle will decrease.

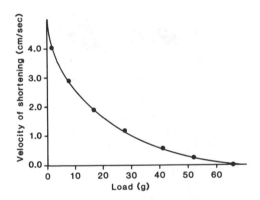

Figure 2   The force-velocity curve of a frog sartorius muscle at 0° centigrade. From ''The Heat of Shortening and the Dynamic Constants of Muscle'' by A.V. Hill, 1938, *Proceedings of the Royal Society of London*, **126**, pp. 136-195. Reprinted with permission.

Muscle Activity Patterns

Prior to any discussion on alterations of the bicycle or changes made in riding position, it is important to review the actions of the major muscles in the leg primarily responsible for the transfer of energy from the rider to the bike. Figure 3 taken from Gregor, Green, and Garhammer (1982) illustrates the average activity pattern of eight muscles in the leg while cycling at 85 rpm against a moderate work load. Of the eight muscles analyzed (see Figure 4), four are two-joint muscles and four are one-joint muscles (see Table 1). The subjects consisted of 10 competitive male cyclists riding a bicycle adjusted to their own personal comfort.

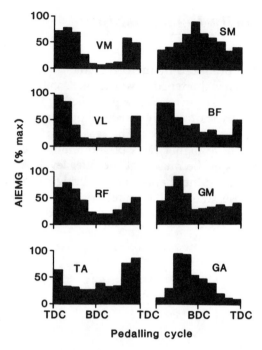

Figure 3   Mean normalized EMGs from 10 subjects. From "An Electromyographic Analysis of Selected Muscle Activity in Elite Competitive Cyclists" by R.J. Gregor, D. Green, & J.J. Garhammer, 1982. In A. Morecki, K. Fidelus, K. Kedzior, & A. Wit (Eds.), *Biomechanics VII* (pp. 537-541), Baltimore: University Park Press.

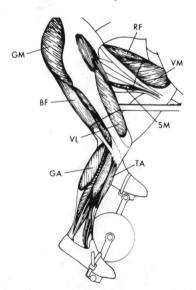

Figure 4   Some of the major lower-extremity muscles used during cycling: gluteus maximus (GM), biceps femoris (BF), vastus lateralis (VL), gastrocnemius (GA), tibialis anterior (TA), semimembranosus (SM), vastus medialis (VM), rectus femoris (RF).

Table 1   Some of the Major Lower-Extremity Muscles Used During Cycling

| Joint | Flexion | | Extension | |
	1 Joint	2 Joint	1 Joint	2 Joint
Hip		RF	GM	BF, SM
Knee		BF, SM, GA	VL, VM	RF
Ankle	TA			GA

Note. From *The Physiology and Biomechanics of Cycling* (p. 41) by I.E. Faria and P.R. Cavanagh, 1978, New York: John Wiley & Sons. Reprinted with permission.

In general we see that six of the eight muscles are very active (greater than 50% of maximum activity) during the first half of propulsion (0° to 90°). Although the quadriceps (knee extensors) then decline in activity, the hamstrings, gastrocnemius, and gluteus maximus continue substantial activity until bottom dead center, the completion of the propulsive phase. Although the kinetics of cycling will be discussed in chapter 5, Figure 5 illustrates the relationship between muscle activity in the leg and the propulsive torques at the hip, knee, and ankle. Significant hip, knee, and ankle extension (as indicated by large curved arrows) are observed in the early phase of propulsion. This occurs in the presence of a great amount of muscle activity (dark gray) and a large propulsive force seen at the pedal. A much broader discussion of this relationship is presented by Gregor, Cavanagh, and LaFortune (1985). The message here is that many variables must be considered together (i.e., muscle activity, propulsive forces and torques, pedal forces, and leg position) to better understand the interaction between rider and bicycle.

Changes in saddle height obviously affect the range of motion each leg must go through when powering the bicycle. These changes influence the length changes experienced by the muscles and, from our previous discussion, subsequently affect their force-production capability. However, the actual magnitude of this length change as related to saddle height alterations is unknown. No study, to date, has related changes in power output or efficiency to specific muscle length changes at varying saddle heights.

Additionally, changes in leg position affect the muscle moment arms at each joint. Joint torques, as previously shown, are in part generated by the muscles in the leg. Because muscles, via attachments to bone, create rotation about joints, any change in their position with respect to the axis of rotation will influence the turning effect of each muscle. Faria and Cavanagh (1978) discuss *competence curves* that combine the effects of length-tension relationships and muscle moment

Figure 5   The relationship between muscle activity in the leg and the propulsive torques at the hip, knee, and ankle.

arms to illustrate the relative ability of each muscle to produce rotation at various joint angles. Although scientific data is difficult to obtain on this topic, the reality to the cyclist is that they do have the ability to change the working range of the legs (i.e., by changing saddle height or crank length), and this will have an effect on their performance.

A remaining question then is, What evidence is there that changes in saddle height affect muscle performance? Desipres (1974) studied muscle activity patterns (EMG) as effected by saddle height and load. Three male cyclists were asked to ride for 30 s at 90 rpm against three different loads and two separate saddle heights. Eight superficial muscles in the leg were sampled at 95% and 105% of pubic-symphysis height. The general conclusions were that as saddle height increased, the leg muscle turned on earlier in the pedaling cycle and stayed on longer. Their magnitudes of activation did not appear larger; they were simply on for a longer period of time. Desipres (1974) also reported that as saddle height increased, the knee showed no appreciable change in its range of motion. However, the ankle went from a 37° range at 95% to a 53° range at 105% of pubic-symphysis height.

If muscle patterns and joint ranges of motion are influenced by saddle height, what can be said about other measures of cycling performance? Thomas (1967) and Hamley and Thomas (1967) presented the results of a study relating power output to saddle-height adjustments. Saddle heights, measured along the seat tube from pedal spindle to saddle crest, were presented as a percent of pubic-symphysis height. They demonstrated that a seat height of 109% was the most effective in power output tests of short duration. Alterations of 4% in saddle height affected power output by approximately 5%. Although tests were conducted on more than 100 skilled riders, no pedaling rates were reported.

In a further evaluation of performance, Nordeen-Snyder (1977) studied the effect of saddle-height adjustments on oxygen consumption and lower limb kinematics in 10 female cyclists. Under steady-state conditions pedaling at 60 rpm against a moderate work load, the results indicate a saddle height of 107% of pubic-symphysis height to require the lowest oxygen consumption. Translated to performance, one might conclude that while 109% is best for short-term power output, 107% appears most efficient for events of longer duration. Nordeen-Snyder (1977) tends to discount this 2% difference, but the 2% difference is equivalent to 1.2 cm at a seat height of 71 cm and 1.7 cm at a seat height of 99 cm.

While saddle-height adjustments affect muscle lengths and should place them in an optimal operating range, pedaling cadence influences the velocities at which these same muscles will contract. In light of our previous discussion on the force-velocity properties of skeletal muscle, we continue, then, to a discussion of pedaling cadence.

Pedaling Cadence

That most competitive cyclists prefer pedaling rates between 80 and 110 rpm has been well documented (Hagberg, Mullin, Giese, & Spitznagel, 1981; Kroon, 1983; Pugh, 1974; Seabury, Adams, & Ramey, 1977; Soden & Adeyefa, 1979; Whitt & Wilson, 1974). Most studies dealing with pedaling efficiency, however, have reported cadences between 33 and 80 rpm (Dickinson, 1929; Gaesser & Brooks, 1975; Pugh, 1974; Seabury et al., 1977). Several explanations may account for these reported differences. Competitive cyclists train using high pedaling rates and are expected to perform more efficiently at these faster rates. Most subjects studied in the past were noncyclists, and the only study to date that has shown higher pedaling rates to be most efficient was also one of the few studies that used competitive cyclists riding their own bicycles (Hagberg et al., 1981).

An additional explanation for the difference in pedaling rates may be attributed to the use of a bicycle ergometer (Seabury et al., 1977). In contrast to an ergometer, the crankset and wheel of a racing bicycle are very light with a significantly lower moment of inertia. For any applied force, then, it is easier to turn the crankset and wheel of a racing bicycle. According to Seabury et al. (1977), if racing bicycles were used instead of ergometers, the most efficient pedaling rates reported might possibly have been higher during work sessions of high power output.

The discrepancies reported in the literature concerning the relationships between cadence, work load, and efficiency may also be attributed to the different methods of calculating efficiency. Because there are different methods for calculating energy expenditure during exercise, efficiency may be expressed as gross, net, work, or delta efficiency (Gaesser & Brooks, 1975). Thus muscular efficiency can be defined in these equations:

$$\text{Gross Efficiency} = \frac{\text{Work Accomplished}}{\text{Energy Expended}} = \frac{W \times 100}{E}$$

$$\text{Net Efficiency} = \frac{\text{Work Accomplished}}{\substack{\text{Energy Expended Above} \\ \text{That at Rest}}} = \frac{W \times 100}{E - e}$$

$$\text{Work Efficiency} = \frac{\text{Work Accomplished}}{\substack{\text{Energy Expended Above That} \\ \text{in Cycling Without a Load}}} = \frac{W \times 100}{El - Eu}$$

$$\text{Delta Efficiency} = \frac{\text{Delta Work Accomplished}}{\text{Delta Energy Expended}} = \frac{\Delta W \times 100}{\Delta E}$$

where W = caloric equivalent of external work performed; E = gross caloric output, including resting metabolism; e = resting caloric output; El = caloric output, loaded cyling; Eu = caloric output, unloaded cycling; ΔW = caloric equivalent of increment in work performed above previous work rate; and ΔE = increment in caloric output above that at previous work rate.

For cycling, it has been documented that, at a constant work load, efficiency decreases with an increase in pedaling speed (Dickinson, 1929; Gaesser & Brooks, 1975). This decrease occurs regardless of the calculation method (Gaesser & Brooks, 1975). The effect of work load on efficiency, however, is dependent on the method of calculation. Both gross (Gaesser & Brooks, 1975; Seabury et al., 1977) and net (Gaesser & Brooks, 1975) efficiency have been shown to increase with power output. In contrast, work efficiency has been reported to remain fairly constant and delta efficiency to decrease with an increase in work load (Gaesser & Brooks, 1975). Regardless of how efficiency is calculated, both work load and pedaling velocity should be considered when calculating a cyclist's most efficient cadence.

Regarding efficiency, a low pedaling cadence should be avoided because of the large energy expenditure in maintaining prolonged contractions (Hartree & Hill, 1928). Although the amount of force increases as the contraction speed decreases, the energy needed to maintain the contraction could eventually neutralize any advantage of the enhanced force production. If the pedaling rate is too high, however, little external work can be performed and energy will be wasted not only in the form of heat but also in overcoming the internal resistance of the muscle (Hartree & Hill, 1928).

One of the first studies to look at the effect of pedaling speed on efficiency was conducted by Dickinson in 1929. The most efficient pedaling rate reported was 33 rpm, well below the values reported for most ergometer studies. In a more recent investigation, Seabury et al. (1977) used 3 subjects riding a bicycle ergometer at pedaling rates between 30 and 120 rpm. They reported that as the work load increased from 40.8 to 326.8 w, the most efficient pedaling rate increased from 42 rpm to 62 rpm (see Figure 6). Additionally, Hagberg et al. (1981)

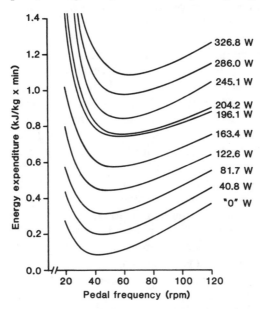

Figure 6 Gross energy expenditure as a function of pedal frequency at 10 constant work loads. From "Influence of Pedalling Rate and Power Output on the Energy Expenditure During Bicycle Ergometry" by J.J. Seabury, W.C. Adams, & M.R. Ramey, 1977, *Ergonomics*, **20**, pp. 491-498. Reprinted with permission.

studied competitive cyclists riding their own racing bikes. For the work load studied, the cyclist's preferred pedaling rates ranged from 72 to 102 rpm. Because this is one of the few studies to analyze pedaling efficiency using competitive cyclists, the following discussion will focus more closely on their results.

The purpose of their investigation was to study the effects of pedaling frequency during submaximal exercise on the cardiovascular, respiratory, metabolic, and perceptual responses of well-trained road-racing cyclists. Each cyclist rode his own racing bicycle on a treadmill to simulate racing conditions. Heart rate (HR), oxygen consumption (VO_2), blood lactate (LA), and a subjective rating of perceived exertion (PE) were some of the major parameters measured.

The cycling consisted of five 5-minute exercise bouts. Each trial was performed with a different gear ratio at a constant speed of 20 mph. The incline of the treadmill was adjusted so that, for each gear used, the work load required approximately 80% of the subject's maximal working capacity. A trial ride was performed by each subject to select what he felt to be his optimal gear ratio for the first work rate tested. Subsequent trials were performed using gear ratios that required two pedaling rates below and two above the cadence of each subject's preferred gear. The pedaling rates tested ranged from 68 to 126 rpm. Exponential increases in oxygen consumption and lactate production were reported both above and below the cyclist's preferred pedaling rate. In contrast, perceived exertion and heart rate increased in a linear fashion from the lowest to highest pedaling rates tested.

According to Hagberg et al. (1981), if a cyclist's most efficient cadence is unknown, he or she should be conservative in his or her estimate and select a cadence slightly below what is believed to be the most efficient. This conclusion is based on the finding that oxygen consumption and lactate production increased at a greater rate above rather than below the preferred pedaling rate. Although track cyclists may reach pedaling rates as high as 160 rpm for brief sprints, pedaling rates above 110 rpm are not recommended for road-racing cyclists (Hagberg et al., 1981). The exponential increase in energy expenditure at these high rates should outweigh any advantage that may result from decreasing the force required per pedal stroke. In terms of maximal power output, pedaling rates in excess of 110 rpm are necessary for short sprints (McCartney, Heigenhauser, & Jones, 1983), but for long-term efficiency, pedaling rates between 80 and 100 should be used (Hagberg et al., 1981).

To this point in our discussion the major focus has been on global measures of performance (e.g., oxygen consumption) in response to different pedaling rates. Considering the exponential increase in energy expenditure both above and below the preferred rate, the following discussion will focus on how muscle fiber type, blood flow, and a cyclist's perception of effort may affect pedaling efficiency.

Muscle Fiber Type

To be successful in competitive road racing, a cyclist should possess both endurance and sprint capabilities. Success in road racing, therefore, should not require a predominance of either fast-twitch (FT) or slow-twitch (ST) fibers. Burke, Cerny, Costill, and Fink (1977) performed muscle biopsies on the vastus lateralis of 29 competitive cyclists, and although they reported a range of 31% to 67% ST fibers, the average fiber composition was approximately 50% ST and 50% FT fibers.

A cyclist's most efficient pedaling rate, however, may be influenced by his or her muscle-fiber type (Hagberg et al., 1981; Suzuki, 1979). According to Goldspink (1978), both ST and FT fibers have an optimal rate of shortening (see Figure 7). ST fibers are more efficient at slow contraction speeds, whereas FT fibers are more efficient at fast contraction rates. Goldspink (1978) also reported that, when each fiber type

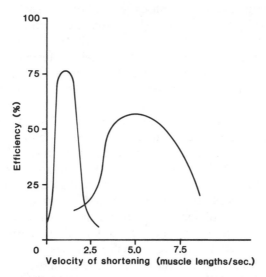

Figure 7 Efficiency (high-energy phosphate into work) of isolated fast and slow muscles at different velocities of shortening. The slow muscle is working most efficiently at a shortening velocity of approximately one muscle length per second, whereas the fast muscle is working most efficiently at a shortening velocity of five muscle lengths per second. From "Energy Turnover During Contraction of Different Types of Muscle" by G. Goldspink, 1978. In E. Asmussen & K. Jorgensen (Eds.), *Biomechanics VI-A* (pp. 27-39), Baltimore: University Park Press.

is shortening at its optimal velocity, an ST fiber is more efficient at shortening and producing work than an FT fiber. It can also be seen from Figure 7 that, although the maximum efficiency is less for FT fibers, the FT fiber can contract with a higher efficiency over a greater range of contraction speeds. The advantage of having a mixed-fiber population, then, is to enable our muscles to contract more efficiently over a greater range of shortening velocities (Goldspink, 1978).

A question that may arise, however, is, How do these findings apply to pedaling efficiency? At low-pedaling rates and low-force outputs we would expect to see a preferential recruitment of ST fibers. With an increase in the pedaling rate and force output, we should see an increase in the recruitment of FT fibers. Because FT fibers in the untrained subject are characterized by a high-glycolytic but low-oxidative capacity, an increase in their recruitment may help explain the increase in lactate production reported above the most efficient pedaling cadence (Gaesser & Brooks, 1975). In most of the studies that analyzed fiber types, however, classification was based on their speed of contraction (i.e., fast or slow) and not on metabolic capacity. This method of classification, therefore, did not take into account those fibers that may have been fast-twitch glycolytic (FG) or fast-twitch high-oxidative glycolytic (FOG). It has been shown that, in response to endurance training of sufficient intensity, FG fibers can achieve the same oxidative capacity as FOG fibers (Edington & Edgerton, 1976). At the high-power outputs used by competitive cyclists, the increase in lactate production at pedaling rates above their preferred cadence may be a more accurate reflection of the metabolic demand placed on the muscles than of fiber recruitment. A high percentage of FOG fibers may help explain not only the high cadence preferred by many competitive cyclists, but also the high efficiency. In addition, the decrease in efficiency above the preferred rate was also attributed to the possibility of an increased recruitment of muscles to help stabilize the trunk (Hagberg et al., 1981). Because the additional muscle mass would contribute minimally to the force output at the pedals, but would increase the oxygen consumption, efficiency should decrease.

The previous discussion dealt with studies that analyzed efficiency of individual muscle fibers, but the study by Suzuki (1979) was one of the first to investigate the relationship between fiber composition and pedaling efficiency. Biopsies were taken from the vastus lateralis muscle of 6 subjects. Three had an average of 78% ST fibers and 3 an average of 76% FT fibers. The exercise protocol consisted of riding a bicycle ergometer at work loads below 80% VO_2max at pedaling rates of 60 and 100 rpm. Suzuki (1979) found that, at 60 rpm, efficiency was unaffected by muscle-fiber type. However, the ST subjects showed a significant drop in efficiency from 60 to 100 rpm, whereas the FT subjects showed an increase in efficiency. More research is, of course, needed in this area, but it must include competitive cyclists riding their own bicycles. These findings, however, do support the hypothesis that a cyclist's most efficient cadence may be influenced by his or her fiber type.

In summary, for submaximal work loads and low-pedaling rates, there appears to be a preferential recruitment of slow-twitch fibers. However, as work load and pedaling rate increase, the recruitment of fast-twitch fibers increases progressively. One explanation is that ST fibers are more efficient than FT fibers at slow contraction speeds, but less efficient at fast contraction speeds (Goldspink, 1978). For the 7 competitive cyclists studied by Hagberg et al. (1981), it was speculated that those cyclists who preferred the higher pedaling rates may have a greater percentage of FT fibers, and those who preferred the lower pedaling rates may have a greater percentage of ST fibers. More research is needed, however, to determine whether the cyclists with the higher preferred pedaling rates do indeed have a greater percentage of FT fibers. A shift in the recruitment of any fiber type will obviously depend not only on the work load and the pedaling rate but also on the trained condition of the cyclist.

Additionally, force-velocity and power curves have been shown to be dependent on the predominant fiber type within a muscle (Tihanyi, Apor, & Fekete, 1982). Figure 8 clearly shows that, for any given velocity, subjects with a higher percentage of FT fibers are able to generate more force during contraction. Because power is the product of force and velocity, it follows that the power output of the

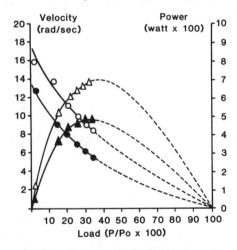

Figure 8 Load-velocity (circles) and load-power (triangles) relationships. Open symbols = fast-twitch (FT) group. Filled symbols = slow-twitch (ST) group. From "Force-Velocity-Power Characteristics and Fiber Composition in Human Knee Extensor Muscles" by J. Tihanyi, P. Apor, & G. Fekete, 1982, *European Journal of Applied Physiology,* **48**, pp. 331-343. Reprinted with permission.

FT group would be higher. It is also evident that a cyclist rich in ST fibers would generate maximum power at a slower pedaling rate than a cyclist rich in FT fibers (Komi, 1984). Muscle fiber composition, therefore, should be considered not only when determining a cyclist's most efficient cadence but also when looking at power output.

Blood Flow

Because blood flow is one of the determinant factors governing the metabolites used for energy and the cause of fatigue during exercise, it too may have an effect on pedaling efficiency. It has been well documented that the rate of blood flow through a contracting skeletal muscle is related to the intensity of the exercise (Barcroft & Millen, 1939; Pirnay, Marechal, Radermecker, & Petit, 1972; Tonneson, 1964). If a low pedaling speed and a high gear are used, the increase in blood vessel occlusion during contraction may cause the oxygen demand to exceed the oxygen supply and therefore increase the muscle's dependence on anaerobic metabolism for energy. The decrease in blood flow would cause not only an increase in lactate production but also a decrease in its removal rate. This alteration in blood flow may help explain the increase in lactate observed by Hagberg et al. (1981) below each cyclist's preferred pedaling rate. The impaired blood flow associated with a low cadence may therefore limit the oxygen supply to the working muscle and the removal of metabolites and may lead to premature fatigue of the muscle.

Perceived Exertion

Most of the studies in the previous discussion dealt only with the physiological parameters that effect pedaling efficiency. The sensation of effort, however, may also play an important role in dictating a cyclist's preferred pedaling cadence. Although our effort sense is largely a subjective state, it has both psychological and physiological components.

Several methods of rating perceived exertion have been reported in the literature, but most of the studies reviewed used the Borg Scale (see Table 2). The standard procedure was to have each subject rate his or her perception of effort either during or immediately after the work task. The exercise protocol usually consisted of having the subject vary his or her pedaling cadence at some preselected work load on an ergometer.

Table 2 Borg Scale: Perceived Exertion Rating (PER)

How Does the Exercise Feel?	Rating
	6
Very, very light	7
	8
Very light	9
	10
Fairly light	11
	12
Somewhat hard	13
	14
Hard	15
	16
Very hard	17
	18
Very, very hard	19
	20

Note. From "Perceived Exertion as an Indicator of Somatic Stress" by G. Borg, 1970, *Scandinavian Journal of Rehabilitative Medicine, 2-3*, pp. 92-98. Reprinted by permission.

The subjective rating of perceived exertion (RPE) during exercise is thought to depend on both central and peripheral feedback (Cafarelli, 1977; Ekblom & Goldbarg, 1971; Noble et al., 1973). The central input is associated primarily with the cardiorespiratory responses to exercise, whereas the peripheral input is associated with the sensation of muscular and joint strain received from the exercising limbs (Cafarelli, 1977; Ekblom & Goldbarg, 1971; Pandolf, Cafarelli, Noble, & Metz, 1972; Pandolf & Noble, 1973). The existence of two inputs appears logical, but their relative contribution to the sensation of effort is still controversial. Although several studies have reported a direct correlation between heart rate and RPE during submaximal exercise (Borg, 1970; Hagberg et al., 1981), several experiments have shown that when subjects exercised under the influence of heat (Pandolf et al., 1972), drugs (Ekblom & Goldbarg, 1971), or hypercapnia (Cafarelli & Noble, 1976), the rating of perceived exertion was independent of the central processes tested. These findings do not refute the existence of a central input, but they do support the hypothesis that the primary signal for the perception of effort is peripheral (Cafarelli & Noble, 1976; Ekblom & Goldbarg, 1971; Noble et al., 1973; Pandolf & Noble, 1973).

When subjects were asked to rate the central and peripheral effort separately during cycling, the peripheral input was usually felt to predominate (Cafarelli, 1977). However, Cafarelli (1977) noted that when subjects reached 50% of their maximal aerobic power, their central input ratings started to increase in relation to the work load. This finding not only helps support the existence of two inputs to the effort sense, but also the conclusion that the central input may become more important as the work load increases.

The relationship between work load, pedaling cadence, and the rating of perceived exertion may be summarized by the findings of Lollgen, Ulmer, Gross, Wilbert, and Nieding (1975). They found that both trained and untrained cyclists preferred a high pedaling cadence for each work load studied. It was also demonstrated that for the higher power outputs, the perception of effort decreased at a greater rate as the pedaling cadence increased (see Figure 9).

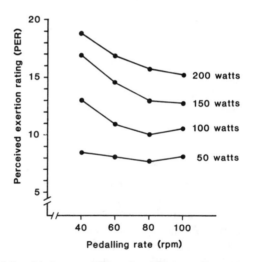

Figure 9   The relationship between PER and pedaling rate. From "Methodical Aspects of Perceived Exertion Rating and Its Relation to Pedaling Rate and Rotating Mass" by H. Lollgen, H.-V. Ulmer, R. Gross, G. Wilbert, & G.V. Nieding, 1975, *European Journal of Applied Physiology, 34,* pp. 205-215. Reprinted with permission.

Summary

In conclusion, pedaling efficiency is dependent on both speed and work load. At slow speeds and low-power outputs, a low cadence is most efficient, but as the speed and power output increase, the most efficient cadence increases (Kroon, 1983; Seabury et al., 1977). It should be clear that a cyclist's most efficient cadence is dependent on several factors:

1. The type of bike being used
2. The rider's position
3. The use or disuse of toe clips and cleated shoes
4. The speed at which the cyclist is riding
5. The gear ratio
6. The rider's trained condition
7. The cyclist's perception of exertion

Because any one of these variables can have a significant effect on pedaling efficiency, they all should be monitored throughout the course of a training program. Likewise, if a significant change occurs in any of these variables, the cyclist's most efficient cadence may need to be recalculated.

Similar arguments pertain to saddle-height adjustment. Although the literature suggests 109% of pubic-symphysis height as optimal for power output and 107% for minimal energy expenditure, no one optimal position exists for all riders. Adjustments certainly affect the muscles responsible for transmitting power to the bicycle, but what is best for each rider is specific to that rider and only continuous testing and trial-and-error experience will ensure maximal performance.

References

Aidley, D.J. (1978). *The physiology of excitable cells*. London: Cambridge University Press.

Åstrand, P.O. (1953). A study of bicycle modifications using a motor driven treadmill. *Arbeitsphysiologie, 15*, 23-32.

Barcroft, H., & Millen, J.L.E. (1939). The blood flow through muscle during sustained contraction. *Journal of Physiology, 97*, 17-31.

Borg, G. (1970). Perceived exertion as an indicator of somatic stress. *Scandinavian Journal of Rehabilitation Medicine, 2*, 92-98.

Burke, E.R., Cerny, F., Costill, D., & Fink,W. (1977). Characteristics of skeletal muscle in competitive cyclists. *Medicine and Science in Sports, 9*, 109-112.

Cafarelli, E. (1977). Peripheral and central inputs to the effort sense during cycling exercise. *European Journal of Applied Physiology, 37*, 181-189.

Cafarelli, E., & Noble, B.J. (1976). The effect of inspired carbon dioxide on subjective estimates of exertion during exercise. *Ergonomics, 19*, 581-589.

Desipres, M. (1974). An electromyographic study of competitive road cycling conditions simulated on a treadmill. In R. Nelson & C. Morehouse (Eds.), *Biomechanics IV* (pp. 349-355). Baltimore: University Park Press.

Dickinson, S. (1929). The efficiency of bicycle-pedalling as affected by speed and load. *Journal of Physiology, 67,* 242-255.

Edington, D.W., & Edgerton, V.R. (1976). *The biology of physical activity.* Boston: Houghton Mifflin Company.

Ekblom, B., & Goldbarg, A.N. (1971). The influence of physical training and other factors on the subjective rating of perceived exertion. *Acta Physiologica Scandinavica, 83,* 399-406.

Faria, I.E., & Cavanagh, P.R. (1978). *The physiology and biomechanics of cycling.* New York: John Wiley.

Gaesser, G.A., & Brooks, G.A. (1975). Muscular efficiency during steady-rate exercise: Effects of speed and work rate. *Journal of Applied Physiology, 38,* 1132-1139.

Goldspink, G. (1978). Energy turnover during contraction of different types of muscle. In E. Asmussen & K. Jorgensen (Eds.), *Biomechanics VI-A* (pp. 27-39). Baltimore: University Park Press.

Gregor, R.J., Cavanagh, P.R., & LaFortune, M. (1985). Knee flexor moments during propulsion in cycling—A creative solution to Lombard's Paradox. *Journal of Biomechanics, 18,* 307-316.

Gregor, R.J., Green, D., & Garhammer, J.J. (1982). An electromyographic analysis of selected muscle activity in elite competitive cyclists. In A. Morecki, K. Fidelus, K. Kedzior, & A. Wit (Eds.), *Biomechanics VII* (pp. 537-541). Baltimore: University Park Press.

Hagberg, J.M., Mullin, J.P., Giese, M.D., & Spitznagel, E. (1981). Effect of pedaling rate on submaximal exercise responses of competitive cyclists. *Journal of Applied Physiology: Respiratory Environmental Exercise Physiology, 51,* 447-451.

Hamley, E.J., & Thomas, V. (1967). Physiological and postural factors in calibration of the bicycle ergometer. *Journal of Physiology, 191,* 55P-57P.

Hartree, W., & Hill, A.V. (1928). The factors determining the maximum work and mechanical efficiency of muscle. *Proceedings of the Royal Society of London, 103,* 234-251.

Hill, A.V. (1938). The heat of shortening and the dynamic constants of muscle. *Proceedings of the Royal Society of London, 126,* 136-195.

Houtz, S.J., & Fischer, F.J. (1959). An analysis of muscle action and joint excursion during exercise on a stationary bicycle. *Journal of Bone and Joint Surgery,* **41-A,** 123-131.

Komi, P.V. (1984). Physiological and biomechanical correlates of muscle function: Effects of muscle structure and stretch-shorten cycle on force and speed. In R.L. Terjung (Ed.), *Exercise and Sport Sciences Reviews,* **12,** 81-121. Lexington, MA: The Collamore Press.

Kroon, H. (1983). The optimum pedaling rate. *Bike Tech,* **2,** 1-5.

Lollgen, H., Ulmer, H.-V., Gross, R., Wilbert, G., & Nieding, G.V. (1975). Methodical aspects of perceived exertion rating and its relation to pedalling rate and rotating mass. *European Journal of Applied Physiology,* **34,** 205-215.

McCartney, N., Heigenhauser, G.J.F., & Jones, N.L. (1983). Power output and fatigue of human muscle in maximal cycling exercise. *Journal of Applied Physiology: Respiratory Environmental Exercise Physiology,* **55,** 218-224.

Noble, B.J., Metz, K.F., Pandolf, K.B., Bell, C.W., Cafarelli, E., & Sime, W.E. (1973). Perceived exertion during walking and running—II. *Medicine and Science in Sports,* **5,** 116-120.

Nordeen-Snyder, K.S. (1977). The effect of bicycle seat height variation upon oxygen consumption and lower limb kinematics. *Medicine and Science in Sports,* **9,** 113-117.

Pandolf, K.B., Cafarelli, E., Noble, B.J., & Metz, K.F. (1972). Perceptual responses during prolonged work. *Perceptual Motor Skills,* **35,** 975-985.

Pandolf, K.B., & Noble, B.J. (1973). The effect of pedaling speed and resistance changes on perceived exertion for equivalent power outputs on the bicycle ergometer. *Medicine and Science in Sports,* **5,** 132-136.

Pirnay, F., Marechal, R., Radermecker, R., & Petit, J.M. (1972). Muscle blood flow during submaximum and maximum exercise on a bicycle ergometer. *Journal of Applied Physiology,* **32,** 210-212.

Pugh, L.G.C.E. (1974). The relation of oxygen intake and speed in competition cycling and comparative observations on the bicycle ergometer. *Journal of Physiology,* **241,** 795-808.

Seabury, J.J., Adams, W.C., & Ramey, M.R. (1977). Influence of pedalling rate and power output on the energy expenditure during bicycle ergometry. *Ergonomics,* **20,** 491-498.

Soden, P.D., & Adeyefa, B.A. (1979). Forces applied to a bicycle during normal cycling. *Journal of Biomechanics*, **12**, 527-541.

Suzuki, Y. (1979). Mechanical efficiency of fast- and slow-twitch muscle fibers in man during cycling. *Journal of Applied Physiology: Respiratory Environmental Exercise Physiology*, **47**, 263-267.

Thomas, V. (1967, June). Scientific setting of saddle position. *American Cycling*, p. 12.

Tihanyi, J., Apor, P., & Fekete, G. (1982). Force-velocity-power characteristics and fiber composition in human knee extensor muscles. *European Journal of Applied Physiology*, **48**, 331-343.

Tonneson, K.H. (1964). Blood flow through muscle during rhythmic contraction measured by 133-xenon. *Scandinavian Journal of Clinical and Laboratory Investigation*, **16**, 646-654.

Whitt, F.R., & Wilson, D.G. (1974). *Bicycling science*. Cambridge: MIT Press.

CHAPTER 5

The Biomechanics of Cycling: Studies of the Pedaling Mechanics of Elite Pursuit Riders

Peter R. Cavanagh
David J. Sanderson
The Pennsylvania State University

Almost all aspects of the study of the mechanics of cycling could be termed biomechanics because the human is an essential part of the mechanical system. Our particular interest in cycling biomechanics is the way in which the rider applies force to propel the system forward. This has been studied by a number of scientists, starting with Scott in 1889, and continuing through the more recent work of Hoes, Binkhorst, Smeekes-Kuyl, and Vissers (1968), Davis and Hull (1981), and a number of studies in our own laboratory (Daly & Cavanagh, 1976; Gregor, Cavanagh, & Lafortune, 1985). The importance of studying the way the rider applies force to the cycle and the limb movements that accompany this force application will never diminish, regardless of the technical advances that are made in the field of equipment design. At each stage in the search for an "ultimate bicycle" the contest will always reduce to the successful application of muscular force to the cycle. The rider will still have a number of alternatives in the way his or her energy is expended.

In this chapter we shall first examine the movement patterns of the legs and then review certain basic concepts in the mechanics of force application and propulsion. The remainder of the chapter will be concerned with the results that we and others have obtained from force and motion measurements on one particular group of cyclists—elite 4,000-m pursuit riders. We have chosen this event because it demands a steady level of effort with a fairly constant pedal rate. Other events, such as sprinting or road riding, would be considerably more challenging to study because of the tactical and environmental factors with which the rider must cope. We shall compare the results from these experimental studies with some current concepts of so-called desirable pedaling mechanics that can be found in the popular cycling literature.

Movements of the Legs

We can gain some appreciation of the limb movements of a cyclist by simply observing the motion, but a better and more quantitative estimate can be obtained from the techniques of cinematography. Using this methodology, specially designed high-speed cameras are used to film athletes in motion. Once the film has been developed and digitized (converted into numbers), a variety of computer techniques are available to calculate joint angles and rates of limb movements. Using cinematography, we have tried to answer some frequently asked questions: How straight is the knee at the bottom of the pedal stroke? Where does maximum knee flexion occur and how much flexion is involved? What is the exact pattern of *ankling*?

We made a series of measurements of the mean values for the extremes of knee and thigh angles of 7 elite pursuit cyclists as they rode at 100 rpm in a 50/13 gear combination. These are shown in Figure 1. It is important to note that measurements were taken during steady-rate pedaling of a racing cycle that the riders had individually adjusted to suit their requirements.

It is interesting, first, to identify the mean ranges of motion that the major joints and segments of the leg go through during one revolution of the crank. The thigh (see Figures 1A and 1B) moves through a 43° arc—from within 19° of the horizontal just after top dead center (TDC) to within 28° of the vertical just before bottom dead center (BDC). During this time the trunk is relatively fixed at an orientation of about 35° from the horizontal. This means that the hip joint never moves into true hip extension that begins when the thigh moves behind the line drawn through the center line of the trunk. There are few other sports where hip motion is as restricted to the flexion part of the range. In moderately fast-speed running, for example, the hip is extended by about 35° and, later in the cycle, is flexed by about 25°. These observations may have important implications for the range over which strength training is performed by cyclists.

Similar observations for the knee joint are contained in Figures 1C and 1D. The mean range of motion for the knee is 74°. Close to BDC the knee is still 37° flexed, whereas just before TDC the maximum

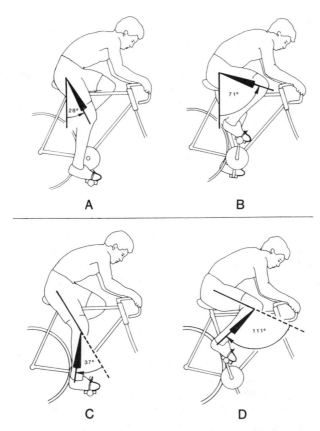

Figure 1 The position of the body and crank at the times of (A) minimum hip flexion and (B) maximum hip flexion, (C) maximum knee extension, and (D) maximum knee flexion. These values are the means from 6 different elite riders who had individually adjusted the cycle to their own requirements. The small, dark-shaded sectors represent the range of values for the particular position found among subjects.

flexion is 111°. The most important observation from these results is that the knee is still considerably flexed at BDC.

On all four diagrams in Figure 1, the variations observed between riders (the range) has been shown as a darkly shaded segment. In all cases this variation is remarkably small—typically about 10°. This suggests that the adjustments the riders have made to the cycle have resulted in fairly standardized body positions once they begin riding. Although the movement patterns are fairly constrained by the geometry of the cycle, some room still exists for variations under different riding conditions. For example, the cyclist can get off the seat and this will, of course, completely alter joint movements. Even while on the saddle, side-to-side movements that occur—for example, in hill climbing—result in slightly different joint and segment motions. These variations have not yet been studied.

Measurements of ankling patterns were also made from the films. Ankling, as used in the vernacular of cycling, does not refer to the ankle-joint angle. Rather it refers to the orientation of the pedal with respect to a reference frame fixed in the cycle (or the vertical on level ground). Our convention for the measurement of the ankling angle is shown in Figure 2. Traditionally, it has been suggested that the heel should be dropped as the pedal moves through the top of the crank revolution (e.g., from 30° before TDC to 30° after TDC) and that the toe should be dropped across the bottom of the revolution (Sloane, 1974). This pattern is shown in Figure 3A.

The mean actual pattern measured from the elite riders in this study is shown in Figure 3B.The pedal orientation dips only slightly below the horizontal (heel-down position), and this occurs not across the top of the cycle but at 90° beyond TDC. The maximum toes-down position actually occurs at about 75° before TDC.

The total pattern that we have measured is shown for one complete crank revolution in Figure 2. The dark solid line is the mean pattern from 7 elite pursuit riders; the two other lines represent values for a single rider. Notice that this rider has an "offset" from the mean pattern for most of the revolution. In general, he keeps his heel a little higher than the mean pattern. This is particularly noticeable on the left side during the recovery phase. There is also an approximate 10° difference in the range of motion on the left and right sides.

Clearly the pattern used by the cyclists shown in Figure 2 (and other nonelite cyclists whom we have studied) departs considerably from what has been accepted in the popular literature. It is likely that the pattern suggested in some lay articles (see Figure 3A) is both anatomically and mechanically impossible if the rider remains in the saddle.

The movement data described above have provided some information on how the movements of the legs are coordinated to provide application of force to the pedals. However, it is important to realize that movement data can never detect changes in the forces applied by the limbs. Imagine, for example, that one of the riders in our film experiment had deliberately started to apply most of the force with the opposite leg. His movement patterns would remain relatively unchanged, but the dynamics of his pedaling action would have changed radically. Much of the remainder of this chapter is concerned with the direct measurement of force application.

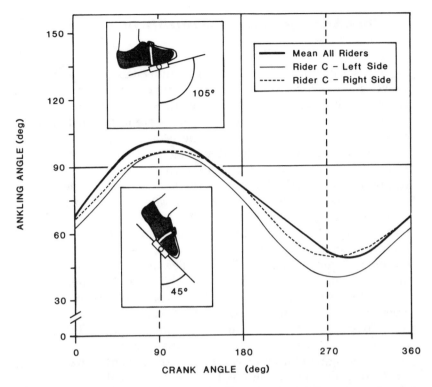

Figure 2 The mean ankling pattern as a function of crank angle for a group of pursuit riders during pedaling at 100 rpm with a power output of 400 W. 0° is the first top dead center (TDC), and 360° is the end of one crank revolution. The inset diagrams show the conventions used for ankling-angle measurements. Also shown on the diagram is the ankling pattern for a particular rider (Rider C). See text for discussion.

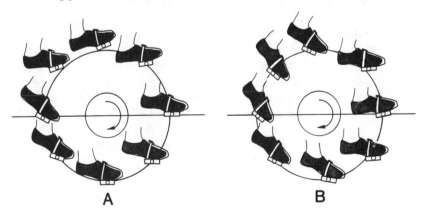

Figure 3 The ankling patterns that are (A) suggested in the popular literature and (B) measured from the elite pursuit riders in our studies. See text for further explanation.

Understanding Forces—Equilibrium

The starting point in an attempt to understand, and perhaps improve, any motion is to examine the forces that cause and sustain it. Newton's classical laws relating force and motion have not lost their validity in the three centuries since they were formulated, and they can help us gain insight into many aspects of cycling. Shown in Figure 4A is a cyclist balancing on the bicycle (e.g., at the beginning of a sprint race). Directly alongside in Figure 4B is what engineers call a free-body diagram of the bicycle. To construct this figure, the bicycle has been drawn isolated from its contact with the rider and the road. At each point of contact, a line called a *force vector* has been drawn. The size and direction of this line is directly proportional to the size and direction of the force acting at that location. Let us look at the various force vectors in Figure 4B: $G1$ and $G2$ are called the ground reaction forces at the rear and front wheels respectively; $P1$ and $P2$ are the forces exerted by the rider on the pedals. These can be directly measured by a device such as that shown in Figure 5. Because the rider is balancing (on a fixed gear), there are equal forces on each pedal. The force Wr is the force exerted by the rider on the saddle due to his or her weight, Wb is the weight of the cycle, and H is the force exerted on the handlebar (shown downward, although it could be in either direction).

Every force in Figure 4B is acting either up or down. No horizontal motion exists because no horizontal forces are acting. This commonsense statement is in fact part of Newton's second law. No vertical motion exists either—not because there are no forces acting (we have identified 7 forces that act vertically)—but because the vertical forces are balanced. The cyclist is said to be in a state of *static equilibrium*. You can see this approximately by comparing the size of the vectors acting up and those acting down. The total length of the saddle, handlebar, weight, and the pedal-force vectors is about the same as the total length of the two ground reaction-force vectors. This actually is a statement of Newton's third law (action and reaction are equal and opposite), and we could analyze Figure 4B mathematically by stating:

$$G1 + G2 = P1 + P2 + Wr + Wb + H$$

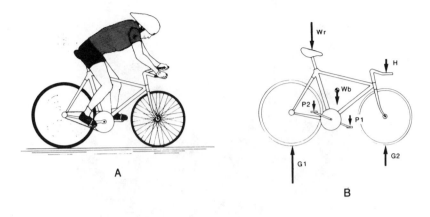

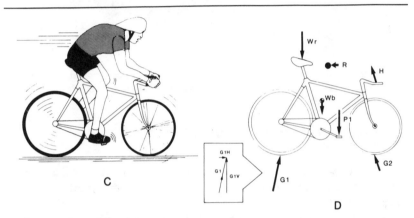

Figure 4 The major forces involved when the rider is (A) balancing on the cycle and (C) propelling the bike forward. The free-body diagrams for these conditions are shown in (B) and (D), respectively. The forces G1 and G2 are the ground reaction forces at the rear and front wheels, P1 and P2 are the left and right pedal forces, Wr is the force due to the weight of the rider, Wb is the weight of the cycle, R is drag due to air resistance, and H is the force exerted by the hands on the handlebars. Note that during balancing (A) and (B) all the forces act in a vertical direction, R is zero, and there are equal forces on both pedals. During riding (C) and (D), G1 now has a component in the direction of propulsion and G2 a component opposing motion. The force G1 is resolved or split into horizontal (G1H) and vertical (G1V) components (inset to D). The horizontal component at the rear wheel (G1H) is the only force propelling the cycle during level riding in still air.

Figure 5 A force-measuring pedal that can monitor the forces applied by the rider. A device to measure the angle of the pedal with respect to the crank is also attached to the end of the pedal.

The Force That Creates Motion

Once the rider starts pedaling, as shown in Figure 4C and in the free-body diagram, Figure 4D, major differences exist in the force situation. First, the forces at the wheels are no longer simply vertical forces. The ground reaction force at the front wheel acts slightly backward because of the rolling resistance of the tire. The force at the rear wheel acts forward because the propulsive force applied by the rider easily overcomes the rolling resistance. Second, we have assumed that $P2$ is zero because the rider is not pushing down during the upward movement. (We shall later show that this assumption may be incorrect.) Third, a new force R has been added to the diagram. This force, acting at the combined center of pressure of rider and cycle, opposes the rider's forward motion and represents the major resisting force—the drag due to air resistance. (The forces due to friction in the bicycle are not considered here.) Notice also that the handlebar force H is now shown as acting upward and backward on the bars, which is the typical riding direction.

As is obvious from Figure 4D, the only force that counteracts both the force resulting from air resistance and the horizontal part of $G2$ is the force at the rear wheel $G1$. Although $G1$ does not act entirely horizontally, it will tend to move the bike forward. To determine the exact amount of forward push that force *G1* will have, we must perform an operation on the force vector called resolving the vector into components. In the insert to Figure 4D, the force *G1* has been shown split into a horizontal part *G1H* and a vertical part *G1V*. The condition for accelerating the bike and rider forward is obviously that the horizontal component *G1H* must be bigger than the resisting forces. Our attention must therefore be focused on how the size of the force *G1H* can be increased with minimum changes in the metabolic cost to the rider. The attempt to diminish the force *R* is obviously also critical, and this is the goal of aerodynamic studies of the cyclist and of his or her equipment and clothing (Kyle, 1986).

In Figure 6 is shown the horizontal component of force at the tire as generated by the forces at the pedal. The only new concept needed to understand this transmission of forces is that of the moment of a force. Force *F1*, which is applied by the rider to the pedal, has a moment about the crank axis equal to the product of the force and its perpendicular distance from the axis of rotation. The cyclist in Figure 6 was pushing vertically down, and the force vector was at right angles to

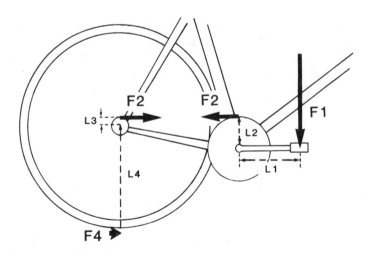

Figure 6 The relationship between pedal force and the horizontal component of force at the rear wheel. *F1* is the pedal force (applied vertically in this example), *F2* is the force transmitted by the chain, and *F4* is the force exerted by the road on the tire (*G1H*). *L1* is crank length, *L2* is the radius of the chainring, *L3* the radius of the rear sprocket, and *L4* the radius of the rear wheel. Under the conditions discussed in the text, the relationship between pedal force and force at the tire is: *F4* = 0.11 × *F1*.

the crank. The moment of the force is therefore calculated directly as the product of force *F1* and crank length *L1*. Stated formally, this is:

$$M1 = F1 \times L1$$

(When the force is not vertical and the crank is not horizontal, the same principles apply, but we must use trigonometry to arrive at the answer.)

Relating Pedal Forces and Wheel Forces

Now that we know the moment of the force that the cyclist is applying, we can determine the force at the rear wheel. The forces caused by the rider, the chain, and the road on the chainset and the rear wheel (ignoring weight and inertial effects) are shown in Figure 6. The moment is the same at all points on the chainring; therefore, we can calculate the force *F2* in the chain because the moment *F2* × *L2* will equal the moment *F1* × *L1*. Notice that *L2* is the radius of the chainring. Therefore, by elementary algebra:

$$F2 = F1 \times L1/L2$$

Now the force *F2* is transmitted directly by the chain to the rear sprocket, which itself has a radius of *L3*. This force therefore has a moment about the rear wheel axis equal to *F2* × *L3*. We are now at the last stage of transmission and can calculate the force at the wheel *F4* by comparing its moment with the moment of the force *F2* just calculated. We can therefore write:

$$F4 \times L4 = F2 \times L3$$

and then

$$F4 = F2 \times L3/L4$$

If we look back over the various expressions, we can actually relate *F4* and *F1* directly with only the various lengths as other items in the equations. The actual expression is as follows:

$$F4 = F1 \times L1 \times L3/L2 \times L4$$

We can now get away from algebraic representation of the lengths and choose some realistic values, as follows:

$L1$ = 17 cm – crank length
$L2$ = 10 cm – chainring radius
$L3$ = 2.25 cm – rear sprocket radius
$L4$ = 35 cm – radius of the rear wheel

We can now rewrite the last equation as:

$$F4 = .11 \times F1$$

In the particular gear that fits the assumptions we have made about the various lengths (approximately 50 × 14), this result means that the force at the wheel will be only 11% of the force at the pedal—a perhaps surprising finding. We effectively have about a 9:1 reduction gear under these conditions. Using similar assumptions about a 42 × 24 gear ratio (that might be used in hill climbing) gives the relationship:

$$F4 = 0.28 \ F1$$

In this case the reduction is only 3.6:1.

This can be verified by turning a bike upside down and experiencing how easy it is to stop the rear wheel from rotating even with a large force applied to the pedal. The implication of our calculations is that the horizontal forces at the wheel are never big. This implies, because we know propulsion is possible, that the size of the resisting forces are even smaller. As a practical example, suppose the cyclist presses vertically down, in the crank position shown in Figure 6, with a force of 200 N (about 45 lb). In a 50 × 14 gear, the horizontal force at the wheel will be about 22 N (5 lb). During level riding in still air, Whitt and Wilson (1982) suggest that this is a reasonable estimate of the average forces a rider must overcome to ride at a speed of 11 m/s (about 25 mph).

Following the forces through the drive chain of the bicycle has served a number of purposes. First, it has introduced some basic operations with forces, and this is appropriate because most of the balance of the chapter will be concerned with forces. Second, it has cast some light on the rather small size of the resisting forces. Eliminating even small additions to the resisting forces will thus have a large percentage effect on the overall resisting force. Finally, it has focused our attention on the forces applied by the rider to the pedal, and we shall now examine these in more detail.

Pedal Forces in More Detail—
Effective and Unused Force

Pedal forces are not always applied vertically and at horizontal crank positions. Shown in Figure 7A is the general case of a force *Fr* applied by the rider to the pedal. Notice that four angles must now be considered:

Θ1—The angle between the crank and the vertical
Θ2—The angle between the axis of the pedal and the vertical
Θ3—The angle between the applied force vector *Fr* and the pedal
Θ4—The angle between the axis of the pedal and the axis of the crank

For the correct calculation of the moment of the applied force about the crank axis, three of these angles must be taken into account.

Let us begin by considering the force vector *Fr* in relation to the pedal. We learned earlier that a force can easily be expressed as two (or more) components. The directions that are chosen for the components are usually at right angles to each other. In Figure 7B we have chosen the directions parallel and perpendicular to the pedal surface. These components *Ft* and *Fn* are called the tangential and normal force components and are defined by the expressions:

$$Ft = Fr \times \cos(\Theta 3)$$
$$Fn = Fr \times \sin(\Theta 3)$$

If you know that the sine of 90° is 1 and the cosine of 90 is 0, then a force applied at right angles to the pedal surface will have no tangential component and will have a normal component equal to the applied force. Resolving forces in these directions only makes "local sense" in terms of the pedal. It tells us how much the rider was pushing or pulling along or parallel to the pedal surface, but unless we take the angles of the pedal and crank with respect to the cycle frame into account, we know nothing about the propulsive effect of the force.

In Figure 7C the same force *Fr* has been divided into components at right angles to and along the axis of the crank. The actual expressions for these components are:

$$Fe = Fr \sin(\Theta 1 + \Theta 2 - \Theta 3)$$
$$Fp = Fr \cos(\Theta 1 + \Theta 2 - \Theta 3)$$

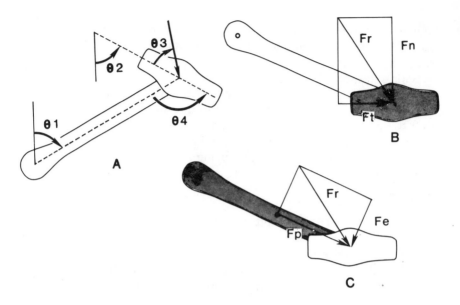

Figure 7   Application of pedal forces. (A) shows the angle conventions used for force calculations. (B) and (C) show the resultant force *Fr* and the various components that can be measured or calculated. In (B), *Fn* and *Ft* are perpendicular to and along the pedal surface, respectively. In (C), *Fe* and *Fp* are at right angles to and along the axis of the crank. *Fe* is called the *effective force* because it represents that component of the resultant force that is effective in generating a force at the rear wheel.

These force components have tremendous relevance to propulsion of the machine and rider as is apparent from a comparison of Figure 7C with Figure 6. It is clear that regardless of crank or pedal position the expression we have derived for *Fe* will always give that component of the applied force that is perpendicular to the crank. This is the component of the force that we need in the calculation of the moment of the applied force about the crank axis, which in turn determines the propulsive force at the wheel.

We have given the force component *Fe* the name *effective force* to characterize its importance in the pedaling process. By convention we give *Fe* a positive sign if it tends to propel the bike forward and a negative sign if it tends to retard pedaling. (Examples of both such cases will be given below.) *Fp*, on the other hand, has no moment about the crank axis because it always has a direction that passes straight through the axis.

By comparing the size of force applied, *Fr*, with the size of effective force, *Fe*, we can define another important quantity, *Fu*, which we call the *unused force*. It is formally defined as follows:

$$Fu = Fr - Fe$$

If the effective force is negative, then all of the force is said to be un-used. (The technically minded should note that Fu is the algebraic difference between the magnitude of the Fr and Fe and not the result of vector subtraction).

It is useful at this point to formally define the torque about the crank. We must remember that the net torque about the crank is the result of forces applied to both the right and left pedals. Sometimes the forces from both sides will add together to produce more torque and sometimes one leg may be producing a *counter torque* (the result of a negative effective force), tending to oppose forward motion. The net torque Tn is defined as:

$$Tn = (Fe \text{ left} + Fe \text{ right}) \times L2$$

where $L2$ is crank length.

Notice that the sign of the effective force will automatically take care of the effects of a counterpropulsive force on the net torque.

Forces That Vary With Time—The Clock Diagram

We have not yet considered the changes in the various forces as the crank rotates through the 360° of the crank revolution. A pictorial representation of typical data obtained from the instrumented bicycle is shown in Figure 8. This represents data for one leg at 20 points in the crank revolution from elite cyclists pedaling at about 100 rpm with close to maximum power output for a steady 4-min ride. We call this presentation a *clock diagram*, and it contains all the information from which subsequent calculations will be made. The crank (dotted line) and pedal (short bold line) are shown in their correct geometric con-figuration and the resultant force vector (bold arrowed line) is shown at each crank position as it was in Figure 7A—except that now the data are real. The size of the force being applied can be estimated by com-paring the length of the force vector at any crank position with the scale of 600 N (about 135 lb) in the right-hand corner of the figure. Our theoretical introduction to pedaling mechanics has led us finally to some real data!

One or two surprising things are seen in this clock diagram. First, the force vector hardly ever has a vertical orientation (a direct push down), as we assumed in some of our earlier discussions. In the first 130° of the cycle, we might describe the force application as a push downward and forward (positions 0 through 7). For much of the re-mainder of the revolution, it is downward and backward. We can also see that the force in Position 4 is close to a 90° angle with the crank

TDC

MEAN ALL RIDERS

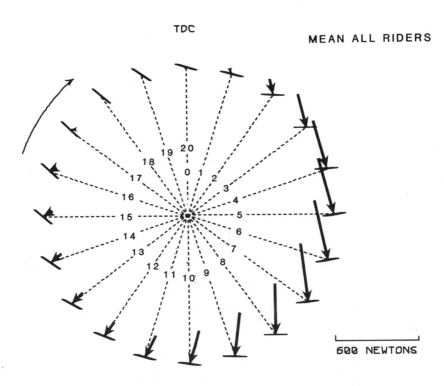

600 NEWTONS

LEFT RESULTANT FORCE

Figure 8 A clock diagram for a group of elite pursuit riders at 100 rpm and 400 W. The orientation of the pedal and the resultant force vector are shown at 20 positions of the crank. Note the orientation of the force vector during the first half of the revolution and the absence of pull-up forces in the second half.

and, in the terms that we defined earlier, probably is close to being 100% effective. From this point, the angle between the resultant force vector and the crank rapidly decreases and, therefore, so does the effectiveness of the force. By the time bottom dead center (BDC) is reached, a fairly large force still exists, but we can see from its orientation that it was not very effective.

Lastly, we should look carefully at the recovery phase. In Positions 10 through 17, a force is still pushing down on the pedals. This will tend to produce a countertorque opposing forward movement and, by our earlier definition, will be a negative-effective force. In particular, note that the rider applies hardly any *pulling-up* force to the pedal under these conditions. Pulling-up force would be shown on the diagram as an arrow underneath the pedal pointing upward. (We shall return to a discussion of this finding later.) Finally, the change in pedal orientation, the ankling pattern, can also be appreciated from Figure

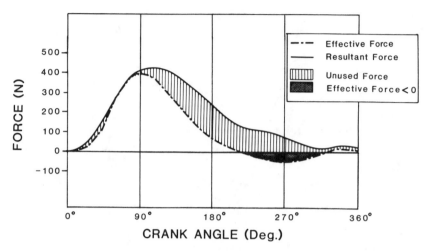

Figure 9 The resultant force (solid line) and the effective force (chain dotted line) for the right leg plotted against crank angle from the same riders and conditions as Figure 8. This display is a continuous one in which the forces at each crank angle are shown. The shaded area represents the force that is not used for propulsion, or the unused force. The effective force peaks at about 90°, whereas the resultant force peaks at 105°.

8. It varies from almost horizontal in Position 3, to a slight heel-down position in Position 6, to a maximum toes-down position in Position 16.

Effective Force and Wheel Force at All Crank Angles

In a typical experiment we usually have much more data than the 20 positions shown in Figure 8. The clock diagram would become unreadable if we added many more crank positions, and so the usual solution is to choose a selection of the variables and plot them on a conventional x-y graph at a large number of crank positions. Such a presentation is made in Figure 9 of the resultant force and the effective force for the same pedaling cycle that was shown in Figure 8. The light-shaded area between the two curves represents the unused force, and the dark-shaded area means that the effective force is negative. In this group of cyclists little difference exists between the resultant and effective forces during the first quadrant. However, the effective force peaks at about 90° and the resultant force peaks about 15° later. Note that there is a considerable amount of unused force (light-shaded area) and that the region of negative effective forces during the recovery phase (dark-shaded area) confirms the impression obtained from the clock diagram.

The profile of the horizontal force at the rear wheel that these applied forces will produce is identical to that of the effective force. Only the scaling is different because of the various factors of gear-crank length, gear ratios, and wheel diameter. The combination of these factors used in the experiment from which the data were collected results in this relationship between *Fe* and *G1H*:

$$G1H = 0.11 \ Fe$$

This relationship permits us to describe how the force at the wheel will vary throughout the crank revolution. The force at the wheel from the right leg is represented by the thin solid line in Figure 10. The dashed line in Figure 10 represents the force at the rear wheel from the other leg. The net effect of both legs is, of course, the algebraic addition (taking into account the minus and plus signs) of both the left and right sides, and this pattern is shown by the bold solid line in Figure 10.

What is not obvious about the total force developed by the riders at the rear wheel is that the force is far from steady. It fluctuates be-

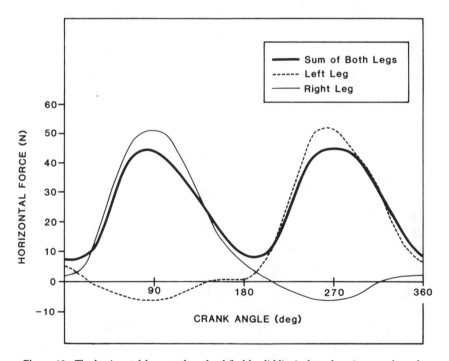

Figure 10   The horizontal force at the wheel (bold solid line) plotted against crank angle in degrees. The force from the right leg (thin solid line) is the result of the effective force shown in Figure 9. The force from the left leg (dashed line) has been added and the net horizontal force at the wheel from the action of both legs is shown as the bold solid line. Note that this force is not constant, or steady, even though the rider feels that the application of force to the pedals is steady. The discrepancy is due to the fact that the resultant force at the pedal is, in general, only partly effective.

tween 8 and 45 N (about 2 and 10 lb). This is definitely not what we, as riders, feel is happening. Our perception is of a smooth and steady force application, but by the time the geometry of force application has been taken into account, the result is rather an uneven propulsive force at the wheel. Because of the inertia that the bike and rider possess, this does not result in large variations in speed during a pedal cycle of fast-level riding. Only when the resisting forces are large (such as in hill climbing) are the within-cycle variations in speed noticeable. As we shall see later, the patterns of force application in such activities are modified to minimize the loss of speed.

The Criterion Diagram

It is frequently useful to divide the crank revolution up into sectors—15° in size, for example—and to make calculations concerning force application in each segment. Summing up the various forces over the segment is achieved by the mathematical technique called integration. When a force is summed over time, the resulting value is known as an impulse. The mean propulsive impulse profile for the group of elite cyclists, obtained by summing the effective force in 15° segments, is shown in Figure 11. This figure gives new insight into

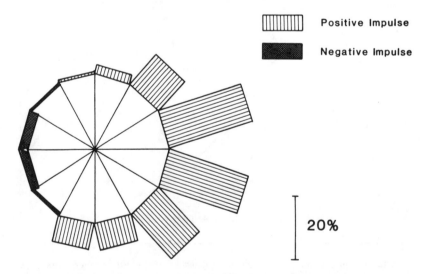

Figure 11 The contributions to propulsion for 12 segments of the crank revolution. The size of each bar represents the percentage of impulse (effective force over time) that the riders exerted in this part of the crank revolution. Note that over 50% of the propulsive impulse is delivered between 60° and 120° after TDC. The scale bar represents 20% of total.

where in the pedal cycle the major propulsive impulse occurs. The forces applied by the cyclists in the third and fourth segments from TDC (between 60° and 120°) together comprise over 55% of the total propulsive impulse applied in the revolution.

Another interesting presentation of the force application in the same crank revolution is the summation of the unused force, as shown in Figure 12. The light-shaded bars on this diagram are simply a segmental representation of the size of the shaded areas that were shown in Figure 9. Only small amounts of force were wasted in the sector of the cycle from 30° before TDC until 90° after TDC. In the next three segments the force wasted becomes much larger, with maximum values on both sides of BDC. During the recovery phase four segments of the graph have been drawn with dark shading projecting inside the diagram. These represent periods when the effective force was negative—tending to oppose the motion. The length of the dark-shaded bars represents the size of the counterproductive effective forces.

The diagram in Figure 12 is called a *criterion diagram* because it has some potential use in helping a cyclist modify his or her patterns of force application. The criterion that the cyclist must attempt to achieve is the minimization of every bar on the criterion diagram without affecting propulsion. Reduction in size of the bars radiating outward from the diagram will mean that less propulsive force is wasted. Reduction

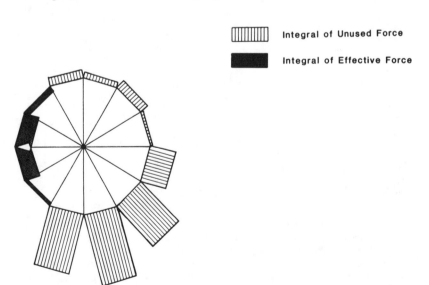

Figure 12   The criterion diagram showing the unused forces (light shading) and negative effective forces (dark shading). The objective for the rider is to reduce the size of the unused force and to eliminate the negative effective forces without decreasing the size of the propulsive impulse.

in the size of the dark-shaded bars projecting into the diagram will eliminate the counterproductive forces that are applied during the recovery phase.

To illustrate the use of these criterion diagrams, two clock diagrams from elite riders with different pedaling styles are shown in Figure 13. Both were collected during steady-state rides of 100 rpm with a power output of about 400 W. Rider A has a remarkable style in which he manages to orient the force vector forward during the last 40° of the downstroke, increasing the effectiveness of the force. The later stages of his recovery phase exhibit small pulling-up forces. Rider B, on the other hand, has more vertically oriented force vectors at the bottom of the downstroke and clearly works against himself in recovery. These features are well illustrated by the criterion diagrams for the two styles in Figure 14. Rider B clearly has to work to reduce the bars representing unused force between 90° and 210° and also to eliminate the negative effective forces between 210° and 330°. Both of these men were extremely successful cyclists, a fact that will later be discussed again in relation to their pedaling styles.

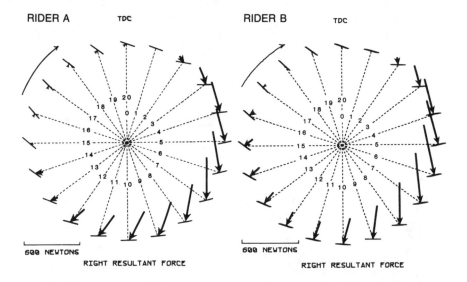

Figure 13   Clock diagrams for 2 elite cyclists with very different styles of pedaling. Rider A sweeps through bottom dead center by orienting his force vector forward. He also pulls up slightly between Positions 16 and 20. Rider B, on the other hand, applies his force more vertically in the region of BDC and, although he does not pull up, he does unload the pedal in Positions 18 through 1.

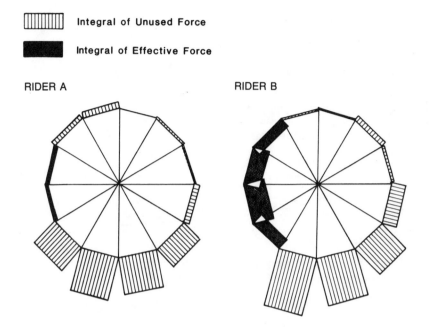

Integral of Unused Force

Integral of Effective Force

RIDER A   RIDER B

Figure 14   Criterion diagrams for the 2 pedal riders shown in Figure 13. Note the contrast in the negative effective forces in the recovery segments between Riders A and B.

Power Output in Cycling

The record books conceal an interesting statement about human power output. In Figure 15A we have plotted the average speed for world-record performances (at the end of the 1984 season) for distances ranging from a 200-m track sprint to a 265-km road race. It is not surprising that the 200-m was much faster than the 4,000-m pursuit, but the explanation of this fact is based on a much more complex theory of energy release at the muscular level.

What is notable about the graph in Figure 15A is that, in races longer than 4 k, not much really changes in the speed at which a rider travels. Physiologically, this implies that we have almost reached a plateau of the rate at which energy can be supplied. Mechanically, this is best expressed in terms of power output, which is proportional to the cube of the speed.

A graph of power output against duration of the ride for champion cyclists is shown in Figure 15B. The unit of power output is the

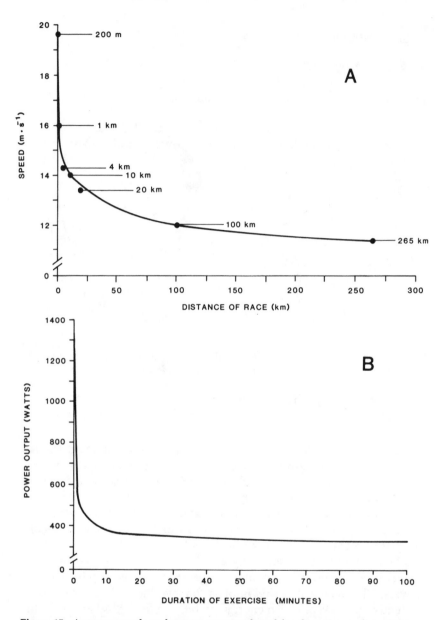

Figure 15 Average speeds and power outputs plotted for champion cyclists. (A) is a graph of average speeds in meters per second of the Amateur World Record holders at the end of the 1984 season at various race distances. Note the small decrement in speed at distances beyond 4 km. (B) is a graph of the maximum power output that can be sustained for work bouts of various durations. A sprinter can generate over 1,300 W for a brief period of time, whereas a road racer has an average power output of less than 400 W. (From Wilkie, 1960)

watt. A sprinter, who only needs to maintain maximum effort for about 10 s, has a power output of about 1,300 W—enough to sustain a medium-sized electric heater for the duration of the effort. A pursuit rider who needs to keep maximum effort for about 4-1/2 min can generate about 400 W—enough to power a small electric drill. Notice that this is only 30% of the sprinter's power output. The 100-km rider can manage an average power output of 300 W—enough to keep three 100 W light bulbs lit. The large gulf in power output occurs early in the distance continuum—between the sprinter and the pursuit rider. The pursuit rider and the 256-km road racer, however, face fairly similar tasks from a power-output perspective. Physiologically, the difference between the sprint and pursuit power outputs is a difference between tasks that are largely supplied by anaerobic energy sources and those supplied mainly by aerobic sources.

The actual power output of a rider in an experimental situation can be measured in a number of ways. The most accurate method involves direct calculation from the forces on the pedal, taking into account the orientation of the forces and the speed of pedaling. This method is preferable to those that measure power dissipated in an external resistance (such as an ergometer flywheel brake) because losses occur at various locations between the pedal and the road, and these would go unmeasured if power were measured externally.

We will examine shortly the different amounts of work done by each leg during a period of pedaling as an important measure of symmetry. Work is done when the cyclist moves against an opposing force—usually the resistance of the air and the frictional and gravitational forces or, in our case, the resistance of the road simulator in the laboratory. Work is entirely independent of the time of the performance. Mechanically, the distinction between work and power is an important one. Power is the rate of doing work. Climbing the same hill twice as fast will result in the same work being done, but the power output will be twice as great (ignoring air resistance as being negligible at low speeds).

Experiments on Symmetry

It might seem reasonable to suggest that cycling would essentially be a symmetrical activity, with each leg making an equal contribution. However, Daly and Cavanagh (1976) showed that in recreational cyclists the relative contributions of each leg were not symmetrical. They further showed that the symmetry of force application was affected by power output and pedaling rate. An understanding of the mechanics of cycling must include an appreciation of the synergistic activity of both legs. With the instrumentation in our lab, we are able to measure the forces applied independently by each leg. Thus, from the two pedals we can measure the relative contribution of each leg to the total force of propulsion. This provides us with the means to assess the symmetry of force application.

We measure two types of symmetry: *force asymmetry* and *work asymmetry*. Force asymmetry is computed on the basis of a comparison of the impulse of the resultant forces that are applied by each leg. The ratio of the right impulse over the left impulse multiplied by 100 gives a relative percentage contribution of each leg and is called the *force-asymmetry ratio*. If the value is greater than 100, the right leg is applying more force than the left, and if the ratio is less than 100, the left is applying more force than the right. This ratio can be considered as a measure of the symmetry of muscular effort. It does not tell us much about propulsion because, as we have seen, the forces are rarely 100% effective in their application. Force asymmetry may reflect bilateral differences in leg strength or perhaps some past injury to either leg.

The *work-asymmetry ratio* is the ratio of the work done by the left leg to the work done by the right leg multiplied by 100. This differs from force asymmetry in that it reflects only the portion of the applied force that contributes to the propulsion of the bicycle, that is, the effective force. Riders may be dominant with opposite legs in work and force asymmetry. This vital point can often provide important clues to the underlying mechanics of pedaling. When the force and work asymmetries are to the same side, the situation is usually fairly straightforward; more work is being done as a result of more force being applied.

If the work and force asymmetries are in opposite directions, the leg producing the most force is doing the least work. The implication is that the forces are being applied to the bicycle less effectively on the side applying more force. The reason might be a previous or existing injury, anatomical variation, neuromuscular deficit, or a training problem. When such asymmetries are encountered, further study is needed on how the training program should be modified.

In our studies with elite cyclists, we have observed a range of force and work asymmetries. At least one cyclist exhibited a force asymmetry of 70%. This rider used the left leg to make a 30% greater contribution to propulsion than the right. This imbalance in the load sharing of the muscles of the leg is likely to lead to poorer performance than when each leg makes an equal contribution. Thus, a cyclist with large asymmetries should endeavor to remove them and strive for a more equal contribution. The cyclist in our studies with the most marked force asymmetry decided to modify both her riding pattern and her off-the-bike training as a result of the finding. Whether in spite of or because of these modifications, she went on to become world champion the next year!

Seat Height and Cleat Position

A topic of great concern to coaches and cyclists is the position of the rider on the cycle. Most coaches believe that minor changes—such as a 5-mm change in the front to back position of the seat—can have a major effect on a cyclist's performance. Few experiments have attempted to examine the effects of such minor changes. The widely held belief is that an optimum seat height exists for which energy consumption at a given power output is minimized. This belief results from experiments in which the seat height was varied by as much as 10 cm.

Nordeen-Snyder (1976) varied the seat height by ±5% of leg length (which she defined as the height of the greater trochanter above the ground). This represented a mean change of about 4 cm for her subjects. Shennum and deVries (1976) used variations of ±12% of inside leg length that resulted in an even greater real variation (10.5 cm). Interestingly, the typical graph relating oxygen uptake to seat height is relatively flat in the region of the optimum. This suggests that a broad region exists in which changes can be made before associated metabolic and biomechanical changes occur. Yet the breadth of this region exceeds the window within which the cyclist would choose to fix his or her saddle.

In all of these experiments, the approach is usually to exaggerate the adjustment so that a larger change can be observed. We then assume that a smaller adjustment will cause a smaller change but in the same direction. This small change may, if measured in isolation, have been below the threshold of experimental error and subject variation. Using a procedure similar to those described, we have collected data on the changes in the mechanics of cycling as seat position was adjusted. We moved the seat up and down, forward and backward by amounts sufficient to elicit significant changes in pedaling mechanics. This was a rather unpopular experiment with our elite cyclists, who complained that changes of this magnitude (4 cm up and down) were both unrealistic and uncomfortable—in some cases actually painful. Muscles were sore and in some cases the riders could not, or were not willing to, complete the ride.

Our results tended to parallel the physiological data. As the seat was moved up and down from the cyclist's chosen position, the effectiveness of pedaling, particularly in the recovery phase, decreased. In our experiment, an increase of 4 cm in seat height resulted in a decrease in the overall effectiveness of 4%. During the recovery segments, the decrease in effectiveness in certain segments was as large as 43%! This raises the possibility that such procedures could be used to help determine optimum seat height, but many more experiments of this nature need to be done. Also, other factors such as the load transmitted by the joints, in particular the knee, are going to have an influence on correct seat height, regardless of metabolic economy or mechanical measures.

A similar experiment involved moving the cleat position on the shoe back and forward from the riders' chosen positions by as much as 2 cm. The results of this experiment were somewhat surprising. Even though the riders perceived large differences between the various conditions, the mechanics of force application remained largely unchanged apart from a predictable shift in the ankling patterns.

In fact, if the criterion of success was whether the riders could push that gear ratio and rpm for the required time under the new conditions, most of the riders were successful. Clearly, a gulf exists between what experienced elite riders know to be the case and what can be observed from pedal-force measurements. None of the riders would have even started a race with the cleat in the extreme position that we used, yet our results demonstrate that they were capable of applying the same force vectors in the same orientation. We can only conclude that a great deal is still to be learned about the optimization of position on the bicycle.

Optimal Pedaling Rate

Most experienced cyclists state without hesitation that their optimal pedaling rate for steady-rate riding is between 90 to 110 rpm. However, frequently they cannot explain why or how they chose this rate. Some of the explanation is historical in nature ("all champion cyclists ride at this rate"), and others say simply that they settled upon this rate naturally. Little data are available on actual pedaling rates during competitions of various durations. The single article we have located (Ulmer, 1970) confirms pedal rates in excess of 110 rpm as being typical in races on the track.

On the other end of the spectrum, novice cyclists typically pedal at lower rpms. If 90 rpm is a critical rate, why must riders learn or develop this rate over time rather than assume it automatically? A number of investigators have shown an optimum pedaling rate indeed exists (Coast & Welch, 1985). Typically, in an experiment to measure optimal pedaling rate, cyclists would ride an ergometer at a set power output with a range of pedaling rates from, for example, 40 rpm to 120 rpm. During these riding periods the energy cost of the ride would be measured by recording the oxygen uptake. The optimal pedaling rate would be the rpm that results in the lowest oxygen uptake for that power output. When this experiment was repeated at a variety of power outputs, Coast and Welch have shown that the optimum rate is dependent on the power output. It appears that the higher the power output, the higher the optimal rate will be.

These findings put into context some of the differing opinions about pedaling rates. Competitive cyclists can work at greater intensities and thus produce higher power outputs than the novice cyclist. Hence, the novice will pedal at a lower power output and have a lower optimal pedaling rate. A question that arises from these data is, How is this notion of optimal pedaling rate reflected in the biomechanics of cycling? This was not one of the questions that we tried to answer in our studies with the elite riders, but we do have some preliminary information from another study on experienced recreational cyclists.

In this study we held the power output constant and recorded biomechanical data while the riders rode at three different pedaling rates (60, 80, and 100 rpm). Preliminary examination of the results indicate relatively larger negative effective-force contributions during the recovery phase at higher rpms. The mechanics of the propulsive phase were similar at both high- and low-pedaling rates (except for proportionately smaller forces at higher rpms). Thus, the faster the rider spins, the more he or she works against him- or herself during recovery. Although these data suggest that changes in the mechanics of cycling are a function of pedal rate, further study is needed on whether these changes are in harmony with the metabolic changes.

Forces During the Recovery Phase—Pulling Up

The experiments described indicate that the energetics of cycling are affected by the mechanics of the recovery phase. This leads to a second issue, that is, whether cyclists pull up during this phase. When asked, most cyclists' response to a question regarding the direction of force application during the recovery phase is usually unequivocal. They say they definitely pull up. This seems contrary to most of the data reported in the literature and the general response of the elite riders whose data we have seen so far. The force-measuring pedal shown earlier (see Figure 5) is obviously ideal to investigate this question. It should reveal that one of three things is happening during the recovery phase: The rider is pushing down, the rider is pulling up, or the pedal is unloaded.

When our measurements determine that the pedal is unloaded, the riders are actually pulling up to some degree. To unload the pedal during the recovery phase, they must overcome two forces. The first is the weight of the leg that gravity is pulling down against the pedal. The second is a force resulting from *inertial effects*—the tendency of the limb mass to resist the motion of the pedal. This second force would be present even in the absence of gravity. Our definition of *pulling up* is when the rider overcomes both of these forces and then applies more force so that an upward force is actually acting on the pedal.

In all of our studies of steady-state riding of the elite 4,000-m pursuit team and of recreational riders, we found only a few examples of pulling up. Some cyclists did exhibit unloading of the pedals during the latter portions of the recovery phase (315° to 360°) but rarely did they pull up. Typically, the pull-up forces, when they existed, were small and applied over a short duration.

These data are certainly contrary to the expressed opinion in a number of magazines suggesting that pulling up on the pedals could result in a 30% increase in efficiency. If changes in economy of riding were to be that large, surely the elite cyclist would pull up. Because no evidence supports the popular claims, we must question why riders in laboratory experiments do not pull up. The literature on this issue has been specific and reproducible over a number of years and in different laboratories. Hoes, Binkhorst, Smeekes-Kuyl, and Vissers (1968), Gregor (1976), and Lafortune, Cavanagh, Valiant, and Burke (1983) have reported the absence of pull-up forces in the recovery phase. The one condition common to all of these investigations is that the riding has been done at a steady rpm with a large inertial load. Although this is similar to high-speed riding on the level, it does not replicate sprinting or climbing hills. The situation regarding pull up will change during these events.

We have conducted one experiment involving a low inertial load. In this case, had the cyclist stopped pedaling, the cycle would also have stopped rapidly. As we can see in Figure 16, the subjects (recreational cyclists) did pull up between Positions 15 and 20 with forces that reached a maximum of approximately 70 N (15 lb). In fact, they did not exert negative torques, even in Positions 10 through 14, where most riders tend to show negative torques (see Figure 4).

Although we know little about pulling up situations that might occur off the track, the question must still be asked, Why, during steady-rate riding, do pursuit riders not pull up during recovery? Presumably,

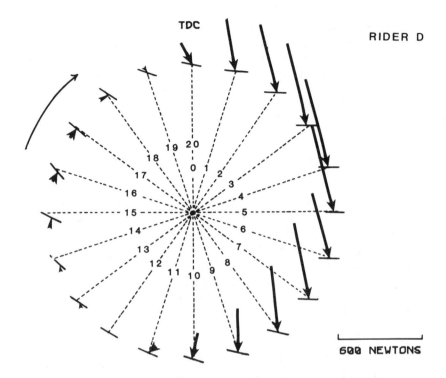

Figure 16 A clock diagram for a recreational rider pedaling against a noninertial load. If he had stopped pedaling, the cycle would have also stopped. Note that the rider applies forces that result in positive torques throughout the pedaling cycle in order to maintain his pedaling rate.

the answer lies in an understanding of the energy cost of pulling up. Earlier, we identified three possible states during recovery. If downward forces are recorded on the pedal, this can be interpreted to mean that the rider is recovering this leg with the aid of the opposite leg. If the pedal is unloaded, the rider is recovering the leg by the action of the leg's own muscular effort. If there is a pull-up force on the pedal, not only is the leg being recovered by muscular action on that side, but the muscular action is in excess of what is needed for recovery and results in propulsive torques.

Each of these three states will likely involve different energy costs. In the absence of clear evidence for the superiority of one style of recovery over another, we have assumed that large negative torques in recovery are undesirable. Because some of the best cyclists in the world do not normally pull up during fast, level, steady-rate riding, we must further assume that it is not economical to do so. Our goal has therefore been to encourage our cyclists to eliminate negative effective forces during recovery without actually pulling up. This issue obviously needs much further study; however, we can say, categorically, that the claims of some that a 30% increase in performance is waiting for all cyclists who pull up is invalid. If the rewards of pulling up were there, one of our elite riders would have claimed them.

Summary

In this chapter we have provided a description of the ways in which elite cyclists propel their machines to victory. The reader will realize that many questions are still unanswered. Principal among these is, Why do some very successful riders have apparently nonoptimal styles? An example from our particular studies has identified Olympic medal winners who have large negative effective forces during the recovery phase. Although it may be argued that elite athletes are examples of self-optimization at work, they might be even better with more optimal riding styles. A particular instance is when large asymmetries are detected.

One thing clear at the elite level is that the significance of averages fades and that each athlete must be examined as a case study. No perfect template, having been measured on elite riders, can be applied broadly to athletes who would emulate their accomplishments. Each case study represents the adaptation of a highly skilled athlete to his or her own anatomical and physiological characteristics. Nevertheless, when an individual rider shows large deviations from the mean pattern, a further examination of riding mechanics is warranted. The scientist and coach must determine whether a particular deviation from the mean is an individual adaptation or whether it should be modified. Much more information and better mathematical models are needed before these decisions can be made objectively.

Some of the criteria for effective pedaling that we have used in the studies reported here represent unachievable goals. For example, with a circular chainwheel arrangement, unused force can never be eliminated completely. Nevertheless, the rider's attempt to do so should result in improved economy of performance. Current experiments are directed toward providing riders with on-line computer feedback to assist them in the modification of their pedaling patterns. We hope that these studies will provide further insight and provide us with a method to allow the technology of biomechanics to have a direct and measurable effect on a rider's performance.

Acknowledgments

This work was supported in part by a grant from the Elite Athlete Program of the United States Olympic Committee. The authors wish to acknowledge the assistance of the following individuals in data collection and processing: Mario Lafortune, John Holden, Rodger Kram, Mary Rodgers, Phil Martin, Dave Petrie, Peter Stothart, Gordon Valiant, and Dawn Ericson. The technical assistance of Joe Johnstonbaugh, Dennis Dunn, Brenda Palmgren, John Palmgren, George Sayers, and Robert Dillon is greatly appreciated. The patience of the athletes who participated in the studies and the encouragement of Ed Burke are also appreciated. Without the willingness of coaches Eddie Borysewicz and Carl Lusenkamp to have their athletes tested, these studies could not have been conducted. Glenn Street made helpful comments on a draft of this chapter.

References

Coast, J.R., & Welch, H.G. (1985). Linear increases in optimal pedal rate with increased power output in cycle ergometry. *European Journal of Applied Physiology and Occupational Physiology,* **53**(4), 339-342.

Daly, D.J., & Cavanagh, P.R. (1976). Asymmetry in bicycle pedalling. *Medicine and Science in Sports,* **8**(3), 204-208.

Davis, R.R., & Hull, M.L. (1981). Measurement of pedal loading in bicycling: II. Analysis and results. *Journal of Biomechanics,* **14**(12), 857-872.

Gregor. (1976). *A biomechanical analysis of lower limb action during cycling at four different loads.* Unpublished doctoral dissertation, The Pennsylvania State University, University Park.

Gregor, R.J., Cavanagh, P.R., & Lafortune, M.A. (1985). Knee flexor moments during propulsion in cycling—A creative solution to Lombard's paradox. *Journal of Biomechanics,* **18**(5), 307-316.

Hamley, E.J., & Thomas, V. (1967). Physiological and postural factors in the calibration of the bicycle ergometer. *Journal of Physiology,* **191**, 55P-57P.

Hoes, M.J.A.J.M., Binkhorst, R.A., Smeekes-Kuyl, A.E.M.C., & Vissers, A.C.A. (1968). Measurement of forces exerted on pedal and crank during work on a bicycle ergometer at different loads.

International Zeitschrift fur Angewandte Physiologie Einschlieslich Arbeitphysiologie, **26**, 33-42.

Hull, M.L., & Davis, R.R. (1981). Measurement of pedal loading in bicycling: I. Instrumentation. *Journal of Biomechanics,* **14**(12), 843-856.

Kyle, C. (1986). Mechanical factors affecting the speed of a cycle. In E. Burke (Ed.), *Science of Cycling* (pp. 123-136). Champaign, IL: Human Kinetics.

Lafortune, M.A., Cavanagh, P.R., Valiant, G.A., & Burke, E.R. (1983). A study of the riding mechanics of elite cyclists. *Medicine and Science in Sports and Exercise,* **15**(2), 113.

Lafortune, M.A., & Cavanagh, P.R. (1983). Effectiveness and efficiency during bicycle riding. In H. Matsui and K. Kobayashi (Eds.), *Biomechanics VIIB: International Series on Sports Science 4B* (pp. 928-936). Champaign, IL: Human Kinetics.

Nordeen-Snyder, K.S. (1977). The effect of bicycle seat height variation upon oxygen consumption and lower limb kinematics. *Medicine and Science in Sports,* **9**(2), 113-117.

Scott, R.P. (1889). *Cycling, art, energy and locomotion.* Philadelphia: J.B. Lippincott.

Shennum, P.L., & deVries, H.A. (1976). The effect of saddle height on oxygen consumption during bicycle ergometer work. *Medicine and Science in Sports,* **8**(2), 119-121.

Sloane, E.A. (1974). *The new complete book of bicycling.* New York: Simon and Schuster.

Ulmer, H.V. (1970). Pedalling speeds of racing cyclists participating in track racing and ergometer riding. *Sportartz und Sportmedizin.*

Whitt, F.R., & Wilson, D.G. (1982). *Bicycling science.* Cambridge: The MIT Press.

Wilkie, D.R. (1960). Man as a source of mechanical power. *Ergonomics,* **3**(1), 1-8.

CHAPTER 6

Mechanical Factors
Affecting the Speed of a Cycle

Chester Kyle
California State University, Long Beach

Certain unavoidable retarding forces act on a cycle. These are air resistance, rolling resistance, friction forces in the power-transmission system, braking forces, inertial forces, and gravity forces (hills). Although each of them has something to do with proper design and choice of equipment, specifics on equipment will be covered in chapter 7. Here we will focus on theory and technique and will aim our discussion at giving the racer a better understanding of what makes a cycle go faster.

The average cyclist probably does not often travel over 15 mph, whereas a well-trained cyclist can travel continuously at over 20 mph. A racing cyclist could exceed 15 mph on almost any kind of a cycle. Realistically, the average cyclist has little to gain by purchasing expensive racing equipment, although many do. If their goal is to go faster, the skill, desire, and athletic ability of the rider could be far more important than equipment, which does not greatly affect the speed of the average cyclist. It can mean winning or losing to a racer, however. At the finish line, an inch is still a winning margin, and proper equipment and technique can easily mean a difference of yards in a race, not mere inches. An understanding of the factors that affect cycle speed will allow a racer to make better choices in technique, equipment, and training methods.

The effort of the rider is by far the most important factor affecting speed. We should therefore briefly review the capability of the human engine to produce power. Almost any adult in reasonable physical condition can deliver 0.1 hp continuously while pedaling a cycle. This is the equivalent of walking about 2 mph or cycling between 12 and 13 mph. The average well-trained cyclist can produce between 0.25 and

0.4 hp continuously. This is the equivalent of cycling from 20 to 24 mph on level ground with no wind. World-champion cyclists can produce nearly 0.6 hp for periods of one hour or more. This is the equivalent of traveling from 27 to 30 mph. Why is it that champion racing cyclists can travel only about twice as fast as a recreational cyclist although they can produce nearly six times as much power? The answer lies in understanding the forces against a cyclist.

Air Resistance

With an ordinary cycle on a level surface with no wind, air resistance becomes greater than all other forces combined at speeds above 10 mph. At speeds above 18 mph, air resistance is more than 80% of the total. At first this may seem quite illogical because air seemingly weighs so little. However, a cyclist traveling at 20 mph will displace about 1,000 lb/min. The machine and rider leave a substantial turbulent wake that costs a large amount of human energy to generate. Two types of aerodynamic drag affect the performance of a cycle, pressure (or form) drag and skin-friction drag. Pressure drag results when the flow of air fails to follow the contours of a moving body. The separation changes the distribution of air pressure on the body, causing a lower pressure on the rearward surfaces than on the forward surfaces and resulting in a drag force. Skin-friction drag results from the viscosity (or stickiness) of the air. Viscosity causes shear forces in the boundary layer of air next to the body. Clothing that ripples or flutters is a visual demonstration of the friction force of the wind.

Blunt shapes such as cylinders, spheres, and other forms found on a cycle are poor aerodynamically because airflow separates from the surfaces. Low-pressure regions form behind the objects, giving a pressure drag that is sometimes hundreds of times greater than the skin-friction drag. In contrast, air flows smoothly around a streamlined shape. The air closes in behind as a streamlined body moves, building up the relative pressure on the rear surfaces. Pressure drag is greatly reduced and skin-friction drag becomes more important. Unfortunately, as a general rule, nothing on a cycle is streamlined. Shown in Table 1 is the wind drag of certain cycle components and accessories at 20 mph.

Aerodynamic drag forces increase as the square of the velocity. (As the speed is doubled, twice as many air molecules are encountered and the rider hits them twice as fast.) Power is proportional to the product of drag force and velocity, so that the power necessary to drive an object through the air increases as the cube of the velocity. Thus,

Table 1   The Aerodynamic Drag of Cycle Components and Equipment:
The Effect of Rider Position, the Drag of Cycle Helmets

Cycle Components and Helmets	Relative Drag
Cycle components—speed 20 mph	
Bare cycle rider in straight-armed racing position	0(reference)
Rider in crouched racing position	−.65 lb (−20%)
Rider in hill-descent position	−.94 lb (−29%)
Cycle plus water bottle	+.10 lb
Cycle plus fenders	+.28 lb
Cycle plus paniers and packs	+.60 lb
Cycle with frame and wheels covered with stretched plastic	−.20 lb
Helmets—speed 30 mph	
Rider with long hair	0 (reference)
Rider plus Cinelli Stap helmet	−.13 lb
Rider plus Brancale helmet	−.26 lb
Best—rider plus aero helmet	
Worst—rider with long hair	

a small increase in speed takes an enormous increase in power. A cyclist who suddenly doubles his power output when he is traveling 20 mph will only increase his speed to about 26 mph. This is the reason for the modest speeds that even the best athlete can reach on a cycle.

The total drag forces against a cycle and rider are shown in Figure 1. As the rider changes position from upright to crouched, the wind resistance decreases dramatically. As the cyclist takes the crouched racing position with the back nearly parallel to the ground, the frontal area of the rider is reduced, and less air is encountered. Also, the shape is more streamlined so that drag is decreased by more than 25%. Cycle racers have been using this awkward, uncomfortable position since before 1900; they would not do this if it were not effective. High speeds on a cycle require high aerodynamic efficiency. Because the human body has a far higher wind resistance than the cycle itself (70% versus 30%), improving rider position is one of the most effective ways of increasing potential speed. Racers should definitely learn to ride in a low-crouched position when solo or at the head of a pack. When in the pack, a slightly more upright position may be more restful.

In descending a hill at high speed, when pedaling is no longer possible, racers often take an efficient low-drag descent position on the cycle so that they can coast as fast as possible. They place both hands together on the upper bars next to the gooseneck and crouch until their chin is nearly touching the gooseneck. The feet are held both at the same level, and the knees are brought together against the upper frame

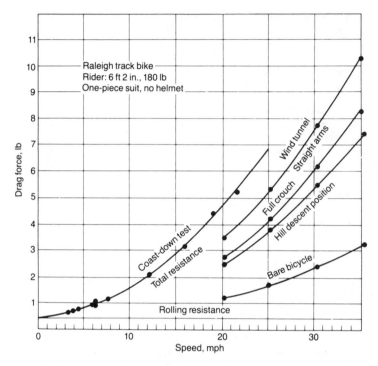

Figure 1 Drag force on a cycle versus speed: The effect of rider position. *Note.* The wind-tunnel measurements are less than the coast-down data because the wheels were stationary and rolling resistance was absent.

tube. In this position, riders can often outcoast others on a hill by several yards.

Drafting

In racing, to learn to draft efficiently in a pace line is essential. Closely drafting riders are in an artificial tail wind that decreases the air drag of those in the rear by more than 40%. Power required is about 30% less for all but the leader in a group of cyclists. The leader uses about the same amount of energy as a solo rider at the same speed. Shown in Table 2 is the decrease in wind resistance as the wheel spacing between cyclists increases. Naturally, the closer they draft, the greater they benefit. Figure 2 shows the wind drag of drafting cyclists as a function of the speed.

In a pace line, or large pack of cyclists, the lead rider can go into oxygen debt and then fall back and rest before taking a turn at the front again. Thus a group can go faster than any single rider in the group,

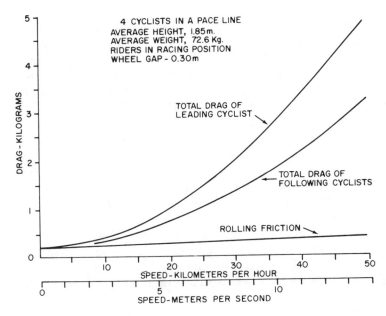

Figure 2 Slipstreaming cyclists: Reduction in wind drag by drafting

Table 2 The Effect of Drafting

Wheel Gap	Decrease in Wind Drag
0.2 m	−44%
0.4 m	−42%
0.6 m	−38%
1.0 m	−34%
1.5 m	−30%
2.0 m	−27%

as long as they are evenly matched. Packs commonly travel from 1 to 3 mph faster than a solo rider over the same distance. Some benefit is derived from drafting even if the cyclist is several bike lengths behind, as long as he or she can find the slipstream. In the 4,000-m individual pursuit on the track, when a following rider is within about 5 bike lengths, suddenly the rider speeds up almost as if being towed, and the pursuit is quickly over. An obvious example of the effect of drafting is the tandem bicycle. Tandems are about 10% faster than a single cycle because the rear rider is in effect drafting close to the front rider. Tandems have 50% less wind resistance than two single cycles. They use 20% less power per rider than two separate cyclists.

In time trialing, if a faster rider passes, the slower rider should pull over slightly into the passing cyclist's draft and speed up somewhat to take advantage of the draft. Although drafting is against the rules in a time trial, if the cyclist stays slightly to one side and behind, it is not obvious. Following slightly behind and to one side of another rider decreases wind resistance by 25% and the rider can maintain a higher speed. Following directly behind, of course, is illegal.

In a crosswind, the racer should try to maneuver to the downwind side of the pack in order to get full benefit of the draft. Riding on the windward side is like riding solo. In a pace line, the line must stagger or form a chevron pattern to take advantage of the shift in the wake. This leads to a common type of accident. The front rider who pulls off downwind is likely to knock down the rear riders who have their wheels overlapping because of the crosswind. The front rider should pull off into the wind even though it seems more logical to seek shelter on the downwind side when dropping back. Under any circumstances, riders should look back before pulling off in order to avoid accidents.

Tail Winds and Head Winds

Since aerodynamic drag is proportional to air velocity squared, head winds, tail winds, and even crosswinds can radically change both aerodynamic drag and power requirements. For instance, a cyclist who wants to continue traveling at 18 mph must increase power input by 100% when riding into a 10-mph head wind. In a head wind, cyclists usually slow down and try to maintain their customary leg force and pedal cadence by shifting gears. Multiple gears are therefore desirable even in level country. In a tail wind, the cyclist merely shifts to a higher gear and goes faster with the customary power output.

With the same power output, head winds will slow down a solo rider about half the wind speed; that is, a 10-mph head wind will slow a rider down about 5 mph. A tail wind will speed the rider up the same amount. However, the increase in speed will not balance the loss in a circuit course. Any wind whatsoever will slow a race that is run around a closed circuit. The reason is that the riders spend half the distance against the wind and not half the time; therefore, a much greater proportion of time is lost against the wind than is gained with the wind. Oddly enough, the drag of a rider increases with a pure crosswind, and so the effect of winds is even worse than it might seem.

Given a choice, a racer always prefers to take his or her turn leading in a tail wind and then to follow in a head wind. Naturally someone must lead into a head wind, and the lead riders usually defensively slow down so as not to burn themselves out. A break seldom succeeds into a head wind because following is so easy; breaking away is much easier downwind, when drafting does not give such an advantage.

The Effect of Altitude

As elevation increases, air density decreases, and thus the wind resistance is less. Thus, bicycle speeds should be much greater at higher altitudes. A countereffect, however, is that the reduced oxygen lessens the endurance of the athlete. Shown in Figure 3 is the variation of air density with altitude along with the theoretical increase of cycle speed with altitude. Some actual race results are plotted; these are less than theory would indicate in all cases. The world 1,000-m record and the hour record were set in Mexico City, elevation 7,400 feet, where the air density is 20% less than at sea level. Cycle speeds at that altitude seem to be from 3% to 5% higher than at sea level. That they are not

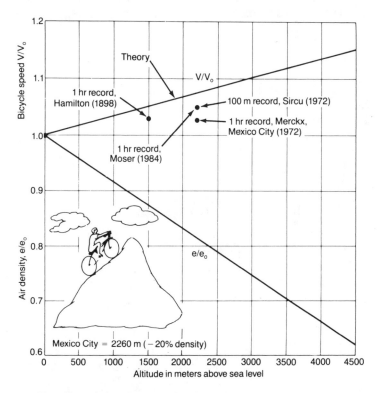

Figure 3 The effect of altitude on air density and cycle speed

about 8% higher, as theory on air-resistance would indicate, is due to the drop in the cyclist's aerobic power.

Surprisingly, the records for the 200-m sprint and for the 4,000-m individual and team pursuit were set at near sea level. Still, for longer distance time trials, speeds definitely increase with elevation. To hold a world-track championship at La Paz, Bolivia, elevation 12,900 ft, where air density is 33% lower than at sea level, would be interesting. If top athletes were present, several world records would surely fall, especially if they were permitted to do a little supercharging with oxygen before the race.

Passing Automotive Traffic

Time-trial speeds are often influenced by passing automotive traffic in an open course. Shown in Figure 4 is the approximate effect on time-trial speed of passing vehicles ranging from small autos to large trucks. The curve was made by observing a consistent time trialist on a level public highway and by using a speedometer accurate to 0.1 mph. Speed

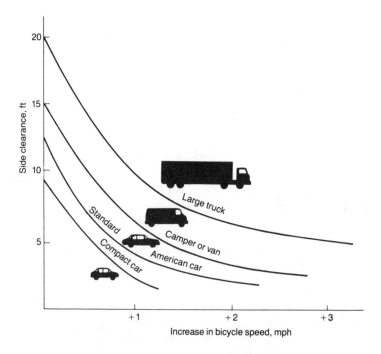

Figure 4 Estimated effect of passing traffic on cycle speed

increases from 0.3 to 3 mph were common as various motorized vehicles passed with about 4 ft of side clearance. Compact cars raised the speed about 0.3 mph, large automobiles about 0.6 mph, and vans and pickup trucks about 1.2 mph. Large highway trucks raised the speed by 2 mph or more. The speed increase lasted about 10 s.

If a strong crosswind was blowing, almost no effect was measured. When passing traffic slowed, approaching the speed of the cyclist, the duration of the effect increased until it sometimes became permanent (i.e., the cyclist was drafting beside the motor vehicle). Naturally, when traffic was heavy, the speed increase was greater. If a steady stream of traffic was passing the cyclist, the speed increased as much as 3 to 5 mph. In time trialing with passing traffic, the cyclist should ride fairly close to the traffic lane for maximum help from the traffic if it can be safely done. If traffic is sparse, every time a car passes, the cyclist can pull over into the wake and receive a boost in speed for several seconds. This tactic can improve time-trial speeds by several seconds and is perfectly legal as long as the cyclist is not obviously drafting a motorized vehicle. The tactic should be practiced with caution because of safety.

Several phenomena related to wind resistance and the cyclist have been mentioned; some are more important than others. Next we will cover some of the other factors affecting cycle speed.

The Effect of Hills

Aside from wind resistance, the most important factor affecting speed is the variation in the surface grade from level. A cyclist who can travel on the level at about 18 mph will slow down to about 6 mph when climbing a 6% grade (a rise of 6 ft in 100 horizontal ft). Down the same hill, the cyclist could travel about 35 mph. Unlike other types of energy mentioned so far, energy used in gaining altitude is not lost (potential energy of elevation), but may be recovered on downhill sections. In a race, however, any hills will slow the race down. The downhill increase in speed will not compensate for the decrease uphill because, as in the wind problem, half the distance is involved rather than half the time.

Typical slopes are shown in Table 3. Shown in Figure 5 is the effect of hills on the speed. If a cycle is on a slope, a weight component exists either with or against the direction of travel. This force is proportional to the slope and to the total weight of the cycle plus rider. The greater the slope and the larger the combined weight of the cycle and the rider, the higher the force of gravity will be.

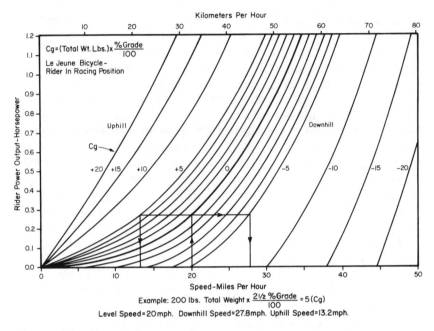

Figure 5   The effect of hills on speed

Table 3   Typical Grades

Terrain	Percent of Grade
Very steep residential streets	20% to 30%
Maximum, modern residential streets	15%
Steep mountain roads	8% to 10%
Normal-limit main highways	5% to 6%
Bridge approaches	3% to 4%

This leads to a seeming paradox. Uphill, additional weight is a handicap, but downhill it is a help. A heavier person can coast faster on the same slope than a lighter person because his or her wind resistance does not increase in direct proportion to weight. One might ask whether a heavier person might perform better in hills than a lighter person. An example using a 200-lb rider and a 160-lb rider, who can both travel 20 mph on the level, shows that on a 5% slope, 1 mi up and 1 mi down, the lighter rider will cover the 2 mi in 7.70 min for an average speed of 15.58 mph. The heavier rider will take 8.58 min for an average speed of 13.99 mph. As one might suspect, it does not pay either to be overweight when climbing hills or to carry extra-equipment weight. This is one reason for the cyclist's traditional pre-occupation with weight saving.

A heavier rider who hopes to keep up with a lighter rider must develop more power. In general, this is possible. The more muscle mass people have, the more powerful they are. Thus the disadvantage of added weight is not as great as it might seem (provided of course that the added weight is muscle and not fat). The conclusion is that probably an optimum body type exists for any particular race circuit. Usually, successful cyclists who race long distances tend to weigh between 150 and 175 lb and to be between 5 ft 8 in. and 6 ft 2 in. tall. Fairly well-defined limits in body size and weight are seen in elite cyclists. Like any other sport, cycling seems to attract those best suited by genetics to compete successfully.

Rolling Resistance

Unlike air resistance, which increases as the square of the velocity, the rolling resistance of cycle tires on a particular surface is nearly constant regardless of the speed. Therefore, as speed increases, rolling drag becomes rapidly less important than wind drag. Typical rolling drag of cycles varies from less than 1/2 lb for fine racing tubular tires (sew-ups) to over 2 lb for balloon tires with knobby tread. Table 4 shows rolling resistance for typical tire types and wheel diameters. The resistances were measured on a smooth surface indoors. Almost no actual data are available showing the effect of road surfaces on rolling resistance. Rolling resistance is hard to measure accurately because it is such a small part of the total drag of a moving cycle. Rolling resistance is almost directly proportional to the total weight on the tire. Table 4 shows a rolling-resistance coefficient *Crr*. To get the total resistance force, multiply this number by the total weight.

The many ways to decrease the rolling resistance of bicycle tires include smoother and harder road surfaces, larger diameter wheels, higher tire pressures, smoother and thinner tread, narrower tires and tread patterns, less weight on the tires, and proper choice of wall and tread material. The cause of rolling resistance is deformation of the wheel, the tire, and the road surface at the contact point. Energy is lost when the wheel, tire, and the surface do not spring back elastically and fail to return all of the energy to the cycle. A tire and wheel and even the road will usually resume their original shape when they

Table 4   The Rolling Resistance of Bicycle Tires on a Smooth Surface

Tire Type	Drag	Weight on Tire	Crr
20 × 2-1/4 in. 45 psi Knobby Tires BMX	2.74 lb	163 lb	.017
27 × 2-1/4 in. 45 psi Knobby Tires BMX	2.27 lb	175 lb	.013
18 × 1-1/4 in. 120 psi Road Sewups 160 gm	1.01 lb	194.4 lb	.0052
20 × 1-1/4 in. 120 psi Road Sewups 180 gm	0.88 lb	195 lb	.0045
27 × 1-1/8 in. 95 psi Road Clinchers	0.78 lb	199 lb	.0039
24 x 1-1/8 in. 120 psi Road Sewups 200 gm	0.73 lb	196 lb	.0037
27 in. × 18 mm 120 psi Road Sewups 160 gm	0.67 lb	196.2 lb	.0034
17-1/4 in. 90 psi Road Clinchers-Moulton	0.68 lb	204.2 lb	.0034
17-1/4 in. 120 psi Road Clinchers-Moulton	0.58 lb	204.2 lb	.0028
27 × 1 in. 120 psi Road Sewups 180 gm	0.58 lb	178.5 lb	.0033
27 in. × 18 mm 120 psi Track Sewups 80-110 gm	0.30-0.50 lb	193.6 lb	.0016-.0026

are not loaded, but internal friction causes deformation energy to generate heat, which is lost to the system. If the road surface is rough, energy can be lost in bounce; if the surface is soft, the tire can actually leave a permanent track. Both of these actions are extremely wasteful of human energy. As stated previously, quantitative data are not available showing the effect of road surface on the rolling resistance of racing tires.

Friction in the Power Transmission System

Gear train and bearing losses with a well-oiled chain absorb only 3% to 5% of the power input. Because this is truly a minor factor affecting cycle speed, the chances for improvement are small compared to overcoming other losses. The cycle drive system is mechanically simple and efficient. Some improvement may be realized by changing the circular pedaling motion to some sort of linear reciprocating motion. The advantage, however, would be in higher human efficiency, not higher mechanical-equipment efficiency. In fact, most systems designed to improve pedaling motion are so complex, unreliable, and inefficient mechanically that they fail completely in their purpose. This is not to say that improvements will not be found; cycle engineers expend much effort each year on designing different transmission systems. Perhaps one of them will succeed, but so far they have generally had disappointing results.

Inertia Forces

Inertia forces in cycling retard acceleration or deceleration and are directly proportional to the total mass and the rate of acceleration. In other words, to accelerate rapidly, a cyclist either must lower the system mass or use a larger force. Rapid acceleration is extremely important in most cycle races, and more money and effort have been spent over the years in lowering cycle weight than on any other item. Elegant alloy racing cycles often weigh less than 18 lb and cost nearly as much as an automobile.

For periods of a few seconds, well-conditioned athletes can put out 1 to 2 hp. A cyclist capable of putting out 1 hp can accelerate from a stop to 25 mph in a calculated 9 s flat (if the combined weight of the cycle and rider is 190 lb). If the same rider adds 2 lb to the cycle, making the total weight 192 lb, it will take about 9.1 s to accelerate to 25 mph. Obviously, if it were only necessary to accelerate once or twice during a race (as in a time trial), this would not be too important. In road races and in some track races, however, acceleration and deceleration are continuous, and the effect is multiplied severalfold. Low equipment weight is important not only in acceleration but, as stated previously, in hills.

Much like the energy used in gaining elevation (potential energy), inertial energy (kinetic energy) can be recovered. Kinetic energy carries a cyclist over a small hill without slowing down and overcomes wind and rolling resistance when a cyclist coasts. However, as with the hills or wind, excess weight has been shown to slow a cyclist down. In addition to retarding acceleration, it increases rolling resistance. Racing cyclists realized this instinctively; they have been shaving weight on racing cycles since their invention in the last century.

Energy Lost in Braking

In any commuting trip or race, a cyclist applies the brakes several times, deliberately wasting the kinetic energy of motion. Moreover, when a cycle turns, the tires apply an effective braking force because of the sideslip of the tires. Unfortunately, little chance exists to recover any of this energy in any simple fashion. Decelerating from 25 mph to a stop squanders enough energy to lift the cycle and rider vertically 21 ft (higher than a two-story building). Cyclists understandably hate to slow down for stop signs or signals. In a race, in order to minimize braking and tire sideslip losses, cyclists should ride in a straight line and try to gauge speed so that braking will not be necessary.

In a typical commuting trip through traffic, braking losses are normally small compared to other losses. They are usually no greater than 8% of the total energy expended by the rider. In a typical training ride of 5 mi at 20 mph, with six stops, wind resistance will absorb 72% of the energy, the tires 15%, braking losses 8%, and bearing and chain losses are 5%.

Summary

This chapter should make obvious where major improvements are possible in cycling. Lowering the wind resistance or rolling drag would provide the best mechanical means of improving race performance. (Improving the condition and skill of the cyclist is of course the most important factor.)

CHAPTER 7

Equipment Design Criteria for the Competitive Cyclist

Chester Kyle
California State University, Long Beach

Little basic research is available to help a competitive cyclist make a logical selection of components and equipment. Most experts will admit that all commercially available racing cycles and components are similar in reliability and performance. Nearly all of the equipment will endure the punishment of a race and, with the right rider, can win. Many ordinary items will perform as well as name brands and cost less than half as much. In this chapter we will use the information presented in chapter 7 to form a logical set of criteria for selecting equipment.

General Equipment Design Criteria

In purchasing equipment, a few things to look for are obvious and some are not. The most common concern of the racer has historically been low equipment weight. This is logical. Not generally known, however, is that rotating components are much more critical than ones that are fixed to the frame. In acceleration, rotating components such as cranks, sprockets, pedals, the chain, and even the shoes have an effective weight greater than their actual weight. The wheels, for instance, have an apparent weight nearly twice the actual. In other words, any weight added to the wheels will have double the effect in added inertia. Because the cranks and chain rotate more slowly than the wheels, their added effective mass is not so much. Still, any savings in weight on rotating components is multiplied in effectiveness.

In the past 10 years, speed records for human-powered vehicles have increased radically because of the use of aerodynamic stream-lining. The record for a standard cycle on the level with no wind is about 43 mph. This was set on a smooth track indoors in a 200-m match sprint between the world's best cycle athletes. Using completely streamlined fully enclosed pedal-powered vehicles, cyclists have reached speeds of over 60 mph. In other words, streamlining works. Because the International Cycling Union (UCI) prohibits any major modification in the standard racing cycle and rider system, only minor aerodynamic improvements are possible. Still, certain things are important in selecting equipment.

Of several ways to lower the wind resistance of cycle equipment, streamlining is the most important. The UCI will permit streamlining of components provided they serve a functional purpose on the cycle. Streamlined tubing, brakes, and rims are common. The practiced eye can recognize shapes that are aerodynamically efficient. Teardrop or oval shapes are best, and sharp corners are to be avoided. If a cycle is carefully streamlined, the aerodynamic drag can be decreased by about 5%. This could mean from 0.3 to nearly 0.7 s improvement in 4,000 m or about 3 to 7 s in 25 mi. Although this does not seem like much, it can mean the winning margin.

Another means of decreasing wind resistance is smoothing of components or decreasing surface roughness. Poor aerodynamic shapes such as bolts, clamps, levers, cables, and posts can all be improved or eliminated by proper cycle design. The object of smoothing components is to avoid sharp edges, corners, rapid changes in contour, or other shapes that might cause air separation or unnecessary turbulence and air resistance. Because rough surfaces cause detrimental air resistance, polished surfaces generally make sense.

One interesting factor that has not been seriously studied is the so-called golf-ball effect. All types of bluff bodies or streamlined shapes such as wings, cylinders, ovals, cubes, or spheres go through an aerodynamic transition at a certain critical speed when the wake changes from laminar to turbulent flow and the drag forces decrease. Below this critical speed smooth shapes are superior, whereas near this speed rough shapes may be better. Streamlined bodies go through a gradual transition but objects such as cylinders abruptly change as the critical speed is exceeded. In wind-tunnel tests, this transition has been noted frequently on cycle components. At racing speeds, cycles have many components that operate around the critical transition point. In this case rough surfaces (like dimples on a golf ball) may be more advantageous than smooth ones that prematurely trip the flow and cause turbulence in the wake. A much lower wind drag could occur. Careful wind tunnel work is required, however, to identify the components that can be improved by utilizing this supercritical flow. This is an area for future research.

Proper location of components can also be important. Given a choice, aerodynamically poor components should be located in the wind shadow or wake of other equipment so that the combined drag will be less. For minimum drag, a clean, streamlined front face is more important than the rear profile. Components such as brakes, cables, and rods should either be hidden in the frame or placed behind other more efficient shapes. A streamlined water-bottle cage can be designed, for example, that presents a smooth profile to the wind when combined with the bottle.

The last simple means of decreasing wind resistance is to lower the frontal area presented to the wind. Because pressure drag normally predominates over friction drag for cycle components, minimum frontal area is important. Components that can be redesigned or oriented differently to give less frontal area will have a lower air drag. A good example is the rider using the uncomfortable egg-shaped body position, which minimizes frontal area. Items such as pumps can be placed parallel to flow (like an arrow) rather than cross to the flow (like a flagpole).

Clothing

Selection of clothing is as important as any other factor in reducing wind resistance. Wind-tunnel tests have shown that sloppy or loose-fitting clothing can raise the total wind drag by 10% or more; hence, more probably can be gained in choosing the proper clothing than by any other legal means in racing. In the 4,000-m pursuit on the track, for example, a drag increase of 0.2 lb slows the racer down by over 2 s. Clothing can easily make this difference. Drag differences of nearly 1 lb have been measured in wind-tunnel tests comparing several clothing combinations.

Wind-tunnel tests have also shown that smooth, shiny materials have a lower wind drag than rough materials. All clothing should closely fit the form without wrinkles or loose material that can flutter in the wind. Racing suits made of stretch materials are expensive but worth the expense. At present the best suits are one-piece "skin" suits without pockets, made from Lycra Spandex. The pattern must be cut so that the suit is wrinkle-free when the rider is in racing position. Because of the variability of the human form, a good market should exist in the future for custom-fitted racing suits. Only a few manufacturers draft patterns for suits that really fit. The Japanese probably produce the best commercially available suit at the moment.

Wind-tunnel tests also show that body hair causes excess wind drag. A person really serious about racing will shave legs and even arms. Hair on the head is also undesirable and should be worn as short as possible or covered with an appropriate helmet. In cold-weather racing, full-length Spandex tights and long sleeves of the same material will serve the same purpose.

Helmets

The helmet is extremely important, and the standard leather "hair net" unfortunately is inferior on almost all counts. First, it really does not absorb heavy shocks. It has a higher wind resistance than almost any other helmet and thus slows the racer down. Finally, the leather helmet usually costs as much or more than another type. Its only advantage is that it rides cooler than a shell type. If it were not for tradition, this helmet would probably have disappeared long ago.

For training, when long hours are spent on the road, sometimes in heavy automobile traffic, a hard helmet with maximum shock protection is a wise choice. Several manufacturers make such a helmet: Bell, MSR, Bailen, and others make a hard-shell helmet with a crushable liner that will absorb considerable impact without injury to the rider. Falling occasionally is part of the sport. Most head injuries caused by falls and other cycle accidents could be avoided by use of a hard-shell helmet.

In racing, most competitors do not wear adequate head protection, partly because of tradition and partly because most good helmets are heavy and hot. Wind-tunnel tests show that a smooth hard-shell helmet is best for speed. Several are available of European manufacture.

For time trialing, in which the cyclist spends long periods at steady-speed riding solo, the best helmets are not presently available commercially in this country. An aerodynamic helmet with a teardrop shape such as those seen in international competition is far superior to any other form of headgear. In a 25-mi time trial, use of an aero helmet would mean about a 30-s improvement in time. Almost all winning time trialists in international competition use aerodynamic helmets, including members of the Russian 100-km, 4-man time-trial team who set the current world record. Aero helmets are not used for protection but for increasing speed. In fact, aero helmets give poor head protection and should not be used other than in time trials. When they become commercially available, however, they will become common even in club time trials.

Shoe, Socks, Pedals, Toe Clips

Socks should be as thin and smooth as possible, of course. When designing shoes, manufacturers unfortunately make no allowance for wind resistance. To compensate for this, international competitors often cover the shoes with Spandex covers that hide the laces and the rough sections of the shoe. Wind-tunnel tests show that covering the laces with tape above the toe clips and straps will lower the wind resistance at 30 mph by about 20 g. This is enough to improve a 4,000-m pursuit time by 0.2 s.

Track racers often bolt their shoes directly to the pedals to cut wind resistance. This is cumbersome but effective. When the toe clips and straps are removed and the laces covered, the drag decreases by about 40 g, or enough to speed up the 4,000-m time by 0.4 s. Because even an inch is a winning margin, international competitors will go to almost any length to improve their times.

In road racing or other types of cycle competition, the results depend more on tactics and teamwork than on equipment. Moreover, cyclists must get off the bike rapidly for tire changes or other reasons so that, if the toe clip and strap are eliminated, a special pedal is required to release the foot rapidly. One commercial pedal of this type is presently available from Cinelli of Italy. A series of so-called aero-pedals is also on the market, but wind-tunnel tests show that some of them have about the same wind resistance as a standard pedal. Most are slightly better, however, and if they are reliable and proven, they can provide a slight advantage.

Tires

Anyone who races will use the lightest, narrowest tubular tires that will stand the punishment of a particular race. On the track where re-rides are allowed for flat tires or in a criterium where mechanical laps are permitted, lighter tires may be used to advantage. In a road race or time trial where flats can lose a race, a heavier tire is logical. Narrow profile tires 16 to 18 mm wide have a lower wind resistance than a standard tire, and they are stronger for their weight than a wider tire. They also weigh less. The only disadvantage is that a narrow tire might give a harder ride. Tire pressure should be as high as is practical. The higher the pressure, the lower the rolling resistance will be. On the track, pressures up to 220 psi are common; on the road, 120 psi is common. Caution is recommended, however. Because high pressure causes blowouts, excess pressure is not wise on the road.

Wheels and Rims

Aero rims give a competitive advantage over a standard rim of about 10 g less air drag per wheel. Flat aero spokes are also better than standard ones. The weight of aero spokes and rims is about the same as that of a standard wheel. They can be used for either track or road racing, and about the only disadvantage is their higher cost.

Small wheels allow the teams to draft closer in a team time trial. They can lower the overall wind resistance of the group enough to make a considerable time difference in races. Wind-tunnel tests show that the drag reduction resulting from drafting closer is about 0.1 to 0.3 lb per rider, which translates into a time improvement of from 1 to 3 s in 4,000 m for a four-man team. Also, the small wheels have a lower wind resistance and weigh less, giving faster acceleration. The only disadvantage to a smaller wheel is a slightly higher rolling resistance. The advantages, however, far outweigh the disadvantages in the case of team time trials.

In international competition 24-in. wheels are becoming common, and 20-in. wheels have been used experimentally. Once superior tires become available for small wheels, the small-wheeled cycles will probably become common even in club time-trial events. In road races, where results do not depend so much on equipment, traditional cycle designs will probably continue to predominate.

Cycle Frames

In choosing a frame, one of the ways to improve race performance is to realize that the critical triangle dimension from seat to handlebars to crank must be set carefully for each rider. Once a rider knows his or her proper riding position, this can be achieved by an enormous number of frame combinations. The critical measurement, for instance, is not the standard frame size, but the correct top tube length, and the seat tube angle and height. A racer should choose the smallest frame size that will give the proper riding position. The reason is that small frames weigh less and have lower wind resistance. Frequently, gooseneck length and height plus seat post length can be adjusted correctly to compensate for a smaller frame size. If the frame is specially made, the length of the top tube and the height of the seat tube can be designed to fit a small frame to a tall rider. This type of custom frame will become more common when riders begin to realize that traditional frame sizing has little to do with the functional value of a cycle.

Since about 1978, so-called aero cycles have become common. Are they of any value? If they are properly designed, yes. Many are really standard in all ways except for slightly flattened tubing in a few places. In wind-tunnel tests, these cycles have about the same drag as a standard cycle. The maker of aero cycles must take great pains to use aero tubing (teardrop shape) that has an efficient shape. If the length-to-width ratio of the tubing cross section is 1.6 to 1, the tubing has a drag that is about 70% of standard round tubing. If the length-to-width ratio is 2.4 to 1, the drag is 38% of round tubing. When the tubing is drafting behind other components (such as the wheels), the drag reduction of the long chord tubing is still superior.

One drawback to an aero frame is the frequent lack of rigidity of the tubing. For racing in which sprints are frequent, such a frame might not be appropriate. Also, aero components sometimes weigh more than ordinary components. Generally, weight can be sacrificed for aero drag reduction, but lack of frame rigidity is a problem that cannot be solved without special frame design.

Components

Most of the components available commercially are so similar that they offer little choice to the racer. In the hopes that at some future date other components will become available, the following wind-tunnel results are presented.

1. *Cranks*—By smoothing the crank arms, removing all rough edges, and forming an oval leading edge on the cranks, the drag can be reduced by about 17 g (0.17 s in 4,000 m).
2. *Sprockets*—A solid disk sprocket has a lower drag than a conventional one by about 5 to 10 g. Holes are not aerodynamically smooth.
3. *Shifters*—In a time trial, the front derailleur is usually unnecessary. If a single shift lever is used, and the lever is smoothed, the aero drag is decreased by about 8 g.
4. *Handlebars*—If aero tubing is used for the horizontal sections of the handlebars facing the wind, the aero drag can be decreased dramatically (as much as 0.2 lb). This is enough to improve 4,000 m times by nearly 3 s.

5. *Seat and Seatpost*—Because the seat and seatpost are drafting between the rider's legs, the shape of the seat makes almost no difference in drag, nor is the shape of the seat post highly important, although an aero shape for the post is desirable.

6. *Water Bottle*—A water bottle is a high-drag item. For example, a normal water bottle and cage adds about 0.1 lb drag to a cycle. By using an aero shape that is smooth and oval (no rough edges), this can be cut in half.

7. *Brake Handles, Derailleurs, Brakes, Et Cetera*—By their nature, these items cannot be streamlined efficiently; however, improvement over what is presently available is certainly possible. In events such as the time trial, the front derailleur may be eliminated. The brakes may be operated with only one handle. Several makes of aero brakes are manufactured, the Modolo probably being the simplest.

8. *Cable and Wire*—Exposed sheathed cable cross to the wind has a drag of about 8 g/in.; this is definitely worth eliminating. Bare brake or shift cable has little drag if kept close to the frame. Cable stops and wire should therefore be used in preference to sheathed cable where possible.

Summary

Bicycle design should be primarily aimed at decreasing wind resistance and weight, whether of clothing or other equipment. Tire rolling resistance (the use of premium sew-up tires) is also of prime importance. To achieve an optimum cycle design suited to an individual rider, almost the only option a serious racer has at present is a custom-made cycle. Despite the tremendous interest in equipment in the racing community, the rider's condition and skill are still the most important factors in winning. If the race is close, however, equipment can make the difference.

CHAPTER 8

Injury Prevention for Cyclists: A Biomechanical Approach

Peter R. Francis
San Diego State University

Understanding the causes and prevention of common pathomechanical injuries sustained by cyclists is very important. Pathomechanical injuries are defined as those injuries that are the results of incompatibilities between the cyclist and the bicycle, rather than injuries sustained by cyclists who fall or collide with other objects while they are riding. The latter injuries are not usually predictable, but they can often be avoided if proper safety equipment is worn, the bicycle is well maintained, and good riding strategies are adopted. Injuries that occur as the result of riding a bicycle that is *not* compatible with the anatomy of the rider are usually predictable. Therefore, an understanding of the mechanics of these injuries is important to all cyclists, whether they ride for exercise, for competition, for transportation purposes, or just for the sheer joy of cycling.

The aim of this chapter is *not* to provide medical diagnoses of specific injuries. If a cyclist suffers a pathomechanical injury caused by cycling, he or she should seek the advice of an individual who specializes in sports medicine. In the past decade our understanding of sport injuries has increased dramatically. Many members of the medical community have come to realize that the area is very specific and is best handled by those who exclusively devote their energies to this area of specialization. In addition, realization that prevention of injury is preferable to medical treatment is growing. Therefore, the aim is to provide cyclists and coaches with an understanding of the mechanical phenomena that cause injuries and to suggest simple techniques that can be used to maintain desirable mechanics.

Why a Biomechanical Approach?

Mechanics is the study of stationary and moving objects and the forces that cause objects to remain stationary or to move. The branch of mechanics that is devoted to the study of living systems (such as the human body) is known as *biomechanics*. Thus any cyclist who is interested in improving cycling performance can benefit from a knowledge of biomechanics. The approach is particularly appropriate for you as a rider or as a coach because you are no doubt mechanically minded. The mechanical similarities between the limbs and joints of the body and some of the components of a bicycle may be readily apparent. The wealth of intuitive understanding gained from assembling and adjusting bicycles has actually provided you with an insight into the mechanics of the human body.

Biomechanics and Modeling

The human body consists of numerous interacting systems that allow the body to utilize oxygen and foodstuffs, excrete waste products, grow in size, reproduce, react to external stimuli, and move from place to place. In the healthy individual the various systems work together in harmony to produce a fairly consistent state of physical and chemical affairs within the organism. Therefore, when trying to understand some of the complexities of human movement, we can often ignore many factors that will "take care of themselves" and can make simplifying assumptions about the way in which the body functions. For example, researchers in biomechanics usually assume that the body can be regarded as nothing more than a set of rigid links that are attached by frictionless joints. Muscles can be considered to be highly efficient machines that forcefully pull on the links so that the links pivot around the joints. It is also assumed that the weight of each link remains constant and that the distribution of the weight of the link does not alter during movement.

In order to check that these are reasonable assumptions, researchers have used computers to try to predict the outcome of exerting forces on the body. A computer is provided with a set of mathematical equations that describe the mechanics of a jointed link system representing a model of the living human body. Theoretical muscular and external forces are then exerted on the model, and the theoretical motions of the model calculated by the computer are compared with the motions of a living human being who has been subjected to equivalent real-world forces. In many cases the theoretical motions of the models are so similar to those of living human beings that the simplifying assumptions incorporated in the models can be concluded to be reasonable.

However, the movements of living human beings can be significantly different from those of an overly simple link system. For example, a link-system model that contains a single large link that represents the thighs, shanks, and feet can effectively predict the effects of external and muscle forces on the motion of a springboard diver while he is in the air performing a simple dive in a fully extended position. However, using several links would be necessary to accurately predict the motions of a diver who changes from a stretched position into a tightly tucked somersault during the execution of a dive. Therefore, the biomechanical technique of using a model to investigate human movement can only be successful if a careful compromise is used. In other words, a model that is too simple cannot accurately predict complex motions, and a model that is too complex will unnecessarily complicate the situation.

With the above reservations in mind, learning much about injuries and injury prevention by examining two different link-system models is possible. An examination of a simple model will provide a superficial understanding of the cycling mechanics of the uninjured cyclist, but a more complex model is needed in order to understand the causes and prevention of common injuries. In either case utilizing complex mathematics is unnecessary; instead, relying upon your mechanical experiences and insight can help in comprehending the simple principles involved.

The Two-Dimensional Model

Components of the Model

Some of the mechanical functions of the human leg can be recognized if we consider it as a simple three-link system (see Figure 1). The rigidity of the thigh is maintained by a single bone, the femur. At the upper end the femur can pivot around the hip joint, and at the lower end the knee joint allows the lower part of the leg (the shank) to pivot on the thigh. The rigidity of the shank is maintained by a pair of parallel bones, the tibia and the fibula. The foot pivots around the lower end of the shank at the ankle joint. At this stage we can assume that the foot can function as a rigid link, and thus the whole of the leg becomes a system of three rigid links. Furthermore, assume that each joint axis is parallel to the other two and perpendicular to the links. We can draw

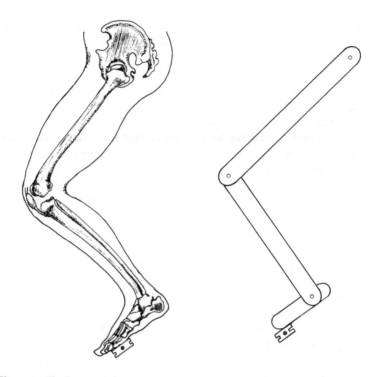

Figure 1 The bones of the leg and the two-dimensional model used to represent the leg of a cyclist

all three links on this flat (two-dimensional) page and imagine that each joint axis is a line pointing out toward you from the paper. Now we can begin to examine the function of the leg during cycling.

Movements of the leg are, of course, brought about by forces exerted by the muscles. Muscles are attached to bones by flexible cords known as tendons. Most tendons are contained in lubricated sheaths that function remarkably like the housings of the brake and gear cables of your bicycle. Tendons are extremely strong and cannot normally be stretched, so powerful muscular forces can be transmitted to precise locations on the bones to cause the body segments to pivot around the joints. An important factor to be remembered is that muscles can only pull, they cannot push. Physiological changes in a muscle can cause the muscle to forcefully shorten in length, and the force of contraction can move adjacent bones toward one another as they pivot around the joint between them. The same muscle cannot now push the two bones away from one another. However, another muscle on the other side of the joint can cause the bones to pivot in the opposite direction, and the original muscle will be passively stretched back to its original length.

Thus when it is necessary to produce a series of repetitive movements, first in one direction and then in the other, a signal is transmitted along a motor nerve to muscle A, which then contracts (see Figure 2). At the same time an inhibiting signal is transmitted to muscle B so that it relaxes as it is passively extended in length. In order to reverse the direction of the motion of the segment the process is reversed. Muscle B receives a motor nerve signal that causes it to contract, while muscle A receives an inhibitory signal so that it will relax as it is being extended. The process is repeated each time the segment completes a back and forth motion.

The type of muscle contractions described above are referred to as *concentric* contractions. When muscles are stimulated they can forcefully shorten in length and cause motion of the body segments. However, muscles are also capable of exerting tension while they are being stretched by external forces. This is known as *eccentric* contraction. For example, if you perform a series of knee bends from a standing position while you are straightening your knees to return to an upright position you will contract the muscles on the front of your thighs in a concentric

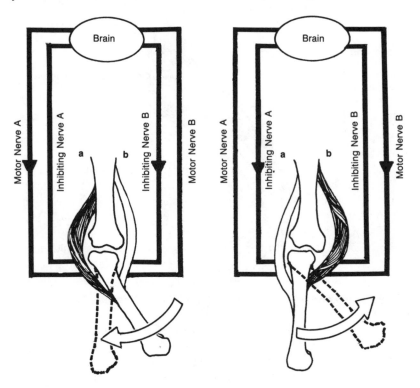

Figure 2 Motor and inhibitory nerve impulses producing movement in one direction and then in the opposite direction

manner. While you are lowering yourself to a squat position you will contract the same muscles eccentrically. The function of the eccentric contraction is to control the rate of descent as you are gradually pulled downward by the weight of your body. If you pause in a half-squat position you will utilize a third type of contraction known as an *isometric* contraction. In this case the active muscles on the front of the thighs will remain the same length while they exert sufficient force to overcome the tendency for your knees to buckle.

Generally, at least two muscles combine to produce a simple movement like flexion or extension at a joint. Each group of muscles ensures that adequate forces can be exerted throughout the full range of motion of the joint and that, in the event of an injury, "back up" muscles will be available to produce motion about the joint. Furthermore, many muscles cross more than one joint so that a muscle may produce motion about more than one joint at a time, or, by selectively stabilizing one joint, the motion may be restricted to the remaining joint or joints.

Figure 3 shows the arrangement of the muscles that produce the important motions of the segments of the leg. Movement of the thigh

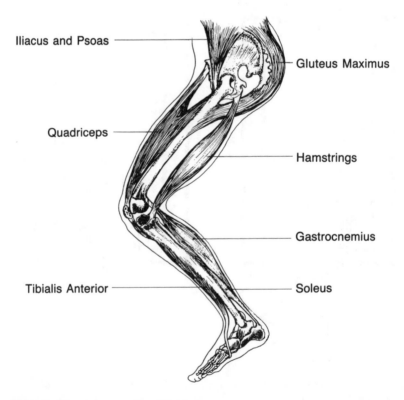

Iliacus and Psoas

Gluteus Maximus

Quadriceps

Hamstrings

Gastrocnemius

Tibialis Anterior

Soleus

Figure 3 The major muscles of the legs

toward the chest is called hip flexion; this can be brought about by the concentric contraction of two large muscles, the iliacus and the psoas. Movement of the thigh in the opposite direction can be produced by contraction of the large muscle that forms the buttocks, the gluteus maximus. This muscle is relatively inactive in the upright position but can contract powerfully when the hip joint is flexed about 90° from the fully extended position. This phenomenon accounts for the increased pedaling forces obtained during hip extension when the rider adopts a flexed position with dropped handlebars. A group of muscles on the back of the thigh produces knee flexion, which moves the heel toward the buttocks. These muscles are known as the hamstrings. (The hamstring muscles also cross the hip joint so that they can also assist the gluteus maximus in extending the hip joint.) Motion in the opposite direction, which extends the knee joint, is produced by contraction of the muscles on the front of the thigh, the quadriceps. (Realize also that one of the quadriceps muscle group also crosses the front of the hip joint so that it can also assist the iliacus and the psoas to flex the hip joint.)

The quadriceps tendon does not connect the quadriceps muscles directly to the tibia. Instead, one section of the tendon attaches the quadriceps to the kneecap and a second section of the tendon attaches the kneecap to the tibia (see Figure 4). The kneecap slides smoothly

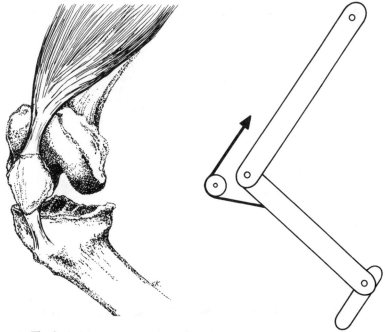

Figure 4 The knee joint represented by a pulley mechanism

into a groove on the end of the femur so that the anatomical structures form a very efficient mechanical system that functions like a pulley. The force of contraction of the quadriceps is transmitted "around the corner" of the flexed knee and is then transmitted to the tibia at an angle that produces forceful knee extension. If the kneecap did not exist, the quadriceps tendon would transmit a force that was almost parallel to that of the tibia. This would produce very weak knee extension.

Movement of the foot toward the shin, which is known as dorsiflexion, is produced primarily by the tibialis anterior muscle, which runs along the outside of the front of the shin. Motion in the opposite direction, pointing the toes, known as plantar flexion, is produced by the soleus and gastrocnemius muscles that make up the calf. (Remember that the gastrocnemius also crosses the knee joint so that it can assist the hamstrings to produce knee flexion.)

We have now examined the actions of the major muscles that cause powerful motions of the segments of the legs. Remember that the actions described are those produced by concentric contraction of those muscles. Bear in mind that flexion at a joint can occur either during the concentric contraction of a muscle designated as a flexor or during the eccentric contraction of a muscle designated as an extensor. Similarly, extension at a joint can occur either during the concentric contraction of a muscle designated as an extensor or during the eccentric contraction of a muscle designated as a flexor. As mentioned earlier,

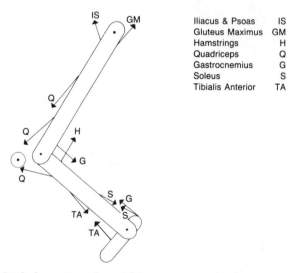

Iliacus & Psoas	IS
Gluteus Maximus	GM
Hamstrings	H
Quadriceps	Q
Gastrocnemius	G
Soleus	S
Tibialis Anterior	TA

Figure 5   Muscle forces exerted on the links of the two-dimensional model

a concentrically contracting muscle will create motion at a joint when the muscle shortens in length. Conversely, when some external force creates motion at a joint, muscles can be used eccentrically to control the rate of pivoting at the joint.

In summary, our two-dimensional model of the lower limb consists of three rigid links. The segments are attached together by frictionless joints, and each joint axis is parallel to the other two and perpendicular to the links. Forces can be exerted on the links, as shown in Figure 5.

Using the Two-Dimensional Model to Study Cycling Mechanics

For the purpose of examining cycling mechanics we can consider the hip joint to be fixed at some location that is determined by the position of the seat of the cyclist. Therefore, the link that represents the thigh can pivot around a fixed axis, the link that represents the shank can pivot around an axis that is attached to the moving end of the thigh link, and the link that represents the foot (and the cycling shoe) can pivot around an axis that is attached to the other end of the shank link. For purposes of simplification, one end of the foot link corresponds to the ankle joint, and the other end corresponds to the point of contact between the pedal and the cycling shoe.

Our model can now be used to produce perfectly efficient propulsion for a bicycle. Needless to say, no human cyclist will ever achieve this lofty goal, but the cyclist who can make changes that more closely approximate the perfect model will improve in performance. In doing so the cyclist will move closer toward his or her own human potential.

In order to produce perfectly efficient propulsion on a conventional bicycle, the model must accomplish three things simultaneously.

1. The end of the foot link that corresponds to the point of contact between the foot and the pedal must move in a perfect circle.
2. The model must exert a constant force on the pedal.
3. The constant force must always be directed tangentially to the circle.

The center of the circle is determined by the location of the bottom bracket of the bicycle, and the radius of the circle is determined by the cyclist's choice of crank length. Although we can readily instruct our model to move the point in a perfect circle, we must remember that it is a highly complex skill for the cyclist. Extensive practice will produce a "motor program," which functions like complex computer software.

The program sends signals to the various muscles that then contract in a precise sequence.

It may be obvious that the model should exert a constant force that is always tangential to the circle. It wastes energy to repeatedly speed up and slow down the pedals. In addition, if part of the force is exerted outward from the circle, the force will tend to stretch the crank, but it will not provide useful propulsion. Conversely, if part of the force is exerted inward from the circle it will tend to compress the crank, but it will not provide useful propulsion. If part of the force is directed from side to side, either toward the bicycle frame or away from the bicycle frame, it will tend to bend the crank sideways, but it will not contribute to propulsion. Finally, if the foot applies torque to the surface of the pedal, the crank will tend to be twisted along its length, but the torque will provide no useful propulsion. No cyclist has unlimited energy to expend, and therefore energy that is used in stretching, compressing, bending, and twisting the cranks will be unavailable for propulsion. If the cyclist can learn to increase the proportion of force that is exerted in a tangential direction, then cycling efficiency will be increased.

Toe clips and cleats assist the rider in maintaining a circular motion of the point of contact between the foot and the pedal, but they do *not* ensure that the force is always directed tangentially. In some instances these devices could encourage a reduced efficiency. For example, if a very unskilled rider has a tendency to exert a sideways force toward the outside of the pedal, the foot may eventually slide off the pedal and motivate the rider to change pedaling technique. If this same rider adds cleats and toe clips, the foot will no longer slide when sideways force is exerted on the pedals, but there is no incentive to make corrections to the inefficient utilization of energy.

On the basis of your experiences as a mechanic, a three-link model that must drive a pedal in a perfect circle may obviously be able to accomplish its objective in many different ways. For example, if the range of motion of the ankle joint is relatively large, the range of motion of the hip joint may be relatively small. Conversely, if the range of motion of the ankle joint is relatively small, then the range of motion of the hip joint may be correspondingly large. In all cases the range of motion of the knee joint will, of course, depend upon the motions of the hip and the ankle. On the other hand, if the ankle joint is locked, the system becomes essentially a two-link model, and only one motion pattern will be able to drive a pedal in a circle.

In order to produce perfectly efficient propulsion using the three-link model, the motions of the three segments must be optimized so that the net effect of the forces that can be applied to the links is maximized. In other words, the best range of motion at each joint will be determined by the availability of propulsive force throughout the system. If the magnitudes of available muscle forces for all combinations of joint angles and speeds of contraction could be determined, then specifying the unique range of motion at each joint that would combine to produce maximum pedaling efficiency would be a relatively simple task. However, due to variations in anatomical and physiological makeup, the information is difficult to obtain and is specific to each individual cyclist. The problem of deriving solutions for all cyclists may therefore be insurmountable. Under these circumstances we are obliged to examine successful performers and attempt to identify characteristics of their performance that may contribute to their success. This approach is based upon the assumption that less successful performers differ from the successful only in their movement patterns. Many other contributing factors are beyond the scope of a biomechanical analysis, and the reader is referred to other chapters of this book for an examination of those factors.

Quite clearly, there is no ideal motion pattern for everyone but examining a highly skilled performer in some detail will be instructive. Figure 6 shows the movement pattern of an Olympic champion

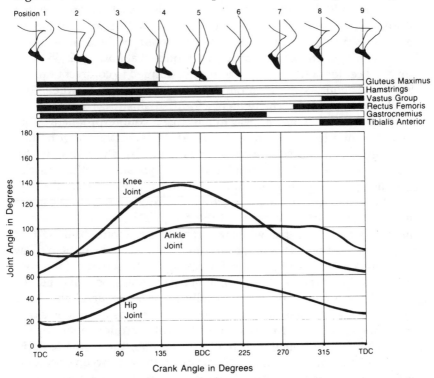

Figure 6 Movement patterns and corresponding muscle activity of a highly skilled cyclist

sprinter. The positions of the thigh, shank, foot, and crank were obtained from high speed cinematography, and the muscle activity information was derived from muscle electrodes connected to an electromyograph. Active muscles are shown in black for each of eight equally spaced positions of the crank.

The angle of the hip joint changed from a minimum of 16° below the horizontal just after the crank was at top dead center, to a maximum of 58° below the horizontal just after the crank was at bottom dead center. Therefore, the total range of motion of the hip joint was 42°. The angle formed by the back of the knee joint changed from a minimum of 63° just before top dead center to an angle of 136° just before bottom dead center. The total knee joint range of motion was therefore 73°. The angle formed by the front of the ankle joint changed from 78° just after the crank reached top dead center to 103° at bottom dead center. Thus the ankle was dorsiflexed at 12° (from an angle of 90°) and subsequently plantar flexed 13°, for a total range of motion of 25°.

Gluteus maximus began to contract at Position 1 (top dead center) and continued to extend the hip joint until just before Position 4. Although the hip continued to extend until just after Position 5 (bottom dead center), this muscle became inactive in the later stage of hip extension. Hip extension was also brought about by the contraction of the hamstrings. These muscles began to contract at Position 2 (45° after top dead center of the crank), and they continued to contract until the crank was about 25° past bottom dead center (midway between Position 5 and Position 6). The tendency for the hamstrings to extend the hip after Position 5 may appear to have been counterproductive, but the same muscles were acting as powerful knee flexors after bottom dead center. Of course, the hamstrings were also attempting to flex the knee joint between Position 2 and Position 5, and so other muscles were used to overcome this tendency in this range of the crank cycle.

The vastus muscles are powerful knee extensors, and we can see that they were active in much of the range in question. The vastus muscles began to contract when the crank was at about Position 8 (45° before top dead center), and they continued their activity until midway between Position 3 and Position 4. Once again the activity of the knee extensors before top dead center may seem counterproductive, but the muscles were contracting eccentrically in order to decelerate knee flexion so that the transition to knee extension was accomplished as smoothly as possible. Knee extension was also brought about by the contraction of the remaining quadricep muscle, the rectus femoris. However, this muscle began to contract midway between Position 7 and Position 8 and it continued to be active until the crank was at about

Position 2. The activity in rectus femoris that occurred before top dead center would have tended to extend the knee, but it would have also tended to flex the hip joint, as described earlier. The contribution of rectus femoris as a hip flexor before top dead center can be regarded as a positive contribution to propulsion, and the same contraction simultaneously decelerated knee flexion prior to the smooth transition to extension. Knee flexion was also brought about by the action of the gastrocnemius, which was active for a considerable proportion of the crank cycle. Gastrocnemius activity began just after top dead center, and it continued until midway between Position 6 and Position 7. The contribution to propulsion after bottom dead center may be obvious, especially because the cyclist was able to exert forces on the toe clip and cleat. The activity in the gastrocnemius between top dead center and bottom dead center appears to have been responsible for plantar flexion of the ankle joint. Dorsiflexion of the ankle occurred from Position 8 until the crank reached top dead center, and therefore, the major dorsiflexor (tibialis anterior) became active from Position 8 until the crank reached top dead center.

The above description is incomplete due to the omission of an examination of other muscles that contribute to the complex motions of the leg. In addition, significant forces due to the inertia of the segments are exerted upon the joints. For example, at any moment in time the shank segment is moving from one place to another, and it is also rotating. At that time the thigh and foot segments must exert forces on each end of the shank to change its velocity so that its motion is constrained within the three-link system. Thus the motion of the shank is determined by muscle forces and the forces of interaction with the other segments. A complete analysis is beyond the scope of this book, but an understanding of muscle activity is a major factor in comprehending the mechanics of cycling.

The Three-Dimensional Model

You will recall that the two-dimensional model was based on the assumption that each joint axis was parallel to the other two. In effect it was assumed that all three joints were simple "pin joints," which restricted the three links to pivot in a single plane. However, an examination of the skeleton of the lower limb reveals that the mechanical structure of the joints will allow more complex motions than are possible with the two-dimensional model (see Figure 7).

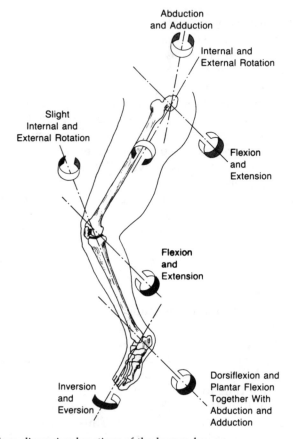

Abduction
and Adduction

Internal and
External Rotation

Slight
Internal and
External Rotation

Flexion
and
Extension

Flexion
and
Extension

Inversion
and
Eversion

Dorsiflexion and
Plantar Flexion
Together With
Abduction and
Adduction

Figure 7   Three-dimensional motions of the human leg

Anatomy of the Hip Joint

The hip joint is a ball and socket joint that will permit pivoting around three distinct axes of rotation. As described earlier, the hip joint will allow the thigh to be moved toward the chest and away from the chest (flexion and extension), but it will also allow the thigh to be moved out to the side, away from the midline of the body. This motion is known as *abduction*. The motion that returns the thigh back toward the midline of the body is known as *adduction*. In addition, the hip joint will allow the thigh to be pivoted around an axis that can be considered to pass along the length of the thigh. External rotation of the hip joints will result in the knees being turned out to the side, whereas internal rotation of the hips will turn the knees toward one another.

Anatomy of the Knee Joint

The knee joint is described as a hinge joint, and it is commonly believed that it will only permit flexion and extension as described earlier. However, a closer look at its structure and function will reveal that the knee also allows the shank to pivot around its long axis to produce a few degrees of internal and external rotation. External rotation occurs naturally during the last few degrees of knee extension. The mechanism is responsible for "locking" the knee joint when it is fully extended. Unlike the hip joint, the knee joint is incapable of adduction and abduction. These motions are prevented by the hinge-and-pulley design of the bony surfaces as well as by the strong ligaments on each side of the knee joint and by the half-moon-shaped cartilages that act as wedges at either side of the joint.

Anatomy of the Ankle Joint

Unlike the two joints described previously, the ankle joint does function like a simple pin joint. However, the axis of the ankle is typically oriented with a slight rearward and downward tilt toward the outside. Thus when the foot is pivoted toward the shin, dorsiflexion is accompanied by slight abduction. Conversely, when the foot is pivoted in the opposite direction, plantar flexion is accompanied by slight adduction.

Anatomy of the Foot and Its Joints

The foot itself is clearly not a rigid link, as it is made up of 26 different bones separated by numerous joints (see Figure 8). This complex construction allows the efficient foot to function as a rigid link when it is required to exert force against the ground or some other object such as a bicycle pedal, but it is also equipped to provide a cushioning effect when the foot is subjected to sudden impacts.

A close examination of the bones of the foot provides an insight into its shock-absorbing qualities. The arch on the inner side of the foot (as seen in Figure 8b) can be likened to a "leaf spring" (Figure 8c). Both the foot and a leaf spring absorb shock by partially flattening and then returning to a curved shape in response to sudden impact loading. The overhead view of the foot shows that the ankle bone (or

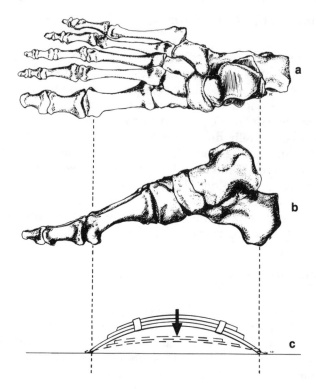

Figure 8 (a) Top view of the bones of the foot; (b) view from the inner side of the bones of the foot; (c) a leaf spring mechanism.

talus) is situated above the inner side of the foot, so that when the shank transmits a load to the foot the inner side of the foot tends to be flattened.

Most of the joints of the foot have very limited ranges of motion, but two joints in particular will allow important motions that are essential to the proper function of the foot. The subtalar joint (and to a lesser extent the midtarsal joint) allows significant rotation of the foot around its long axis. Thus, with your legs stretched out in front of you in a sitting position, the soles of the feet can be turned inward toward one another (this is known as inversion), and to a lesser extent, the soles of the feet can be turned outward away from one another (this is known as eversion). If you attempt to produce the first of these motions you will discover that maximum inversion cannot be accomplished unless you also rotate the feet to a pigeon-toed position (adduction). Simultaneously there is a tendency to plantar flex the ankle joint (see Figure 9). This complex three-dimensional motion is known as *supination*, and it is brought about by the geometry of the ankle, subtalar, and midtarsal joints and by the directions of pull of the extrinsic musculature of the foot. Similarly, you cannot maximally evert the foot unless you also assume a toe out position (abduction). Simultaneously, there is a tendency to dorsiflex the ankle joint. This complex motion consisting of simultaneous eversion, abduction, and dorsiflexion is known as *pronation*.

Finally, an examination of the anatomy of the legs reveals that the joints are not as rigidly confining as those in the field of engineering. Due to the elasticity of some of our tissues and to the "looseness" of the joint structures, living joints can provide slight motion of the components. Obviously, if this motion is excessive the joints become unstable, and serious injuries can occur. Within reasonable limits, however, the cushioning effect provided by the elastic resilience of the joints will help to prevent damage caused by unexpected stresses.

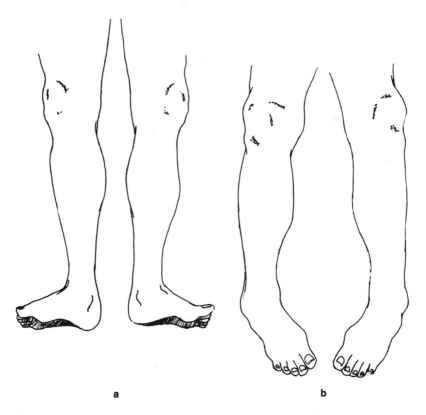

a   b

Figure 9(a) Pronation   **Figure 9(b)** Supination

The Components of the Three-Dimensional Model

In light of the additional complexities of anatomy discussed above, it is possible to utilize a three-dimensional model to examine some of the subtleties of cycling mechanics. The model consists of four rigid links, the "thigh," "shank," "ankle bone," and "foot," which are attached to one another by frictionless joints (see Figure 10). The hip joint will allow a significant range of motion around three different axes, the knee joint will allow a significant range of motion in flexion and extension, and a few degrees of external rotation will be allowed as the knee is fully extended. In addition, a pulley mechanism in front of the knee ensures that forces producing knee extension are exerted in an optimal direction. The axis of the ankle joint is directed slightly rearward and downward toward the outside. The "subtalar" joint (which represents both the subtalar and midtarsal joints of the living foot) will allow inversion and eversion along an axis that runs along the length of the foot. Therefore, the combined motions of the ankle and subtalar joints will allow the complex three-dimensional motions of pronation and supination. Finally, in order to approximate the resilience of a living system, the joints will absorb relatively low levels of compression, tension, bending, shearing, and twisting stresses without sustaining damage.

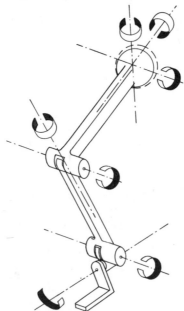

Figure 10 The three-dimensional model

Using the Three-Dimensional Model to Examine Cycling Mechanics

When the three-dimensional model is mounted on a bicycle, the foot link is locked to a pedal by a cleat and toe clip so that its motion is forced to match that of the top surface of the pedal. But, whenever the ankle is plantar flexed, the shank will pivot toward the frame of the bicycle due to the rearward and downward tilt of the "ankle" axis. Fortunately the hip joint will compensate for this motion by slightly adducting the thigh during plantar flexion of the ankle joint. Figure 11 shows a front view of the path of the knee for an Olympic champion sprinter. This international rider does not have a history of lower extremity injuries despite many years of intense training and competition. Therefore, he must have sufficient range of motion and resiliency in the joints to permit these three-dimensional motions without placing damaging stress on his anatomical structures. Furthermore, an examination revealed that the rider had sound foot mechanics so that the

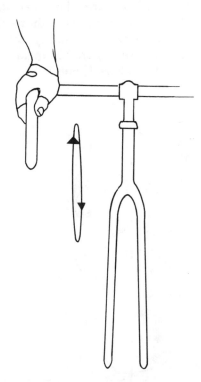

Figure 11 Front view of the path of the tibial tuberosity of a successful cyclist (the tibial tuberosity is the bony prominence on the tibia just below the kneecap)

foot was able to function as an efficient rigid link while it was transmitting forces to the pedal.

Unfortunately, many cyclists are not as mechanically sound as this individual, and they have structural deficiencies that eventually contribute to injuries. An examination of a variety of these deficiencies will give you an insight into both the cause and the prevention of common injuries.

Structural Problems That Can Lead to Injuries

Excessive Pronation. This particular problem may be the cause of more injuries than any other structural abnormality seen in cyclists, and those injuries may appear in any one or more of several different anatomical locations. Recognizing the mechanics involved is especially important so that the rider can learn to take steps to avoid the effects of this potentially devastating problem.

In an ideal foot (sometimes called a neutral foot) the flat base of the heel bone and the flat plane formed by the bottom surfaces of the metatarsal heads (which make up the ball of the foot) are perpendicular to the long axis of the shank when the individual stands comfortably on a flat horizontal surface (see Figure 12). In addition, the combined motion of the subtalar and midtarsal joints will usually permit no more

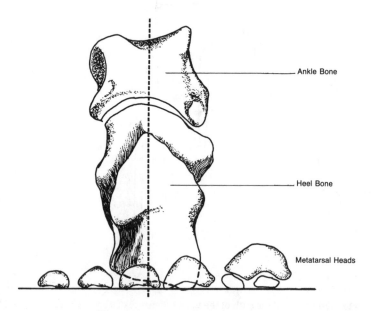

Figure 12   The neutral foot (rear view of the left foot)

than about 20° of inversion and 10° of eversion. Even if the foot is everted through its maximum range the foot will lock to form a rigid link, which can transfer large forces to the pedal of a bicycle.

If we now permit the four-link model to allow a few degrees of frictionless inversion and eversion, we can examine the effects of forces exerted on the foot during pedaling. As you will recall, force transmitted by the shank to the foot will be exerted on the ankle bone, which is situated above the inner side of the foot. This force will therefore tend to evert the foot. This action of eversion will inevitably produce the other component of pronation—that of abduction of the foot. (Remember that it is impossible to maximally evert without also abducting the foot.) However, as the foot is constrained by the cleat and the toe clip, the foot cannot abduct and so the shank is forcibly pivoted inward (see Figure 13). Fortunately, however, the hip joint can compensate for this motion by adducting slightly during maximum loading. As shown in Figure 11, the mechanically sound rider is able to dissipate the stresses involved by producing a characteristic side-to-side motion of the knee, as seen from the front.

In many individuals the foot can evert beyond 10°, especially when the foot is bearing a heavy load. When this happens the lower extremity is subjected to stresses that cannot be dissipated by the resiliency of

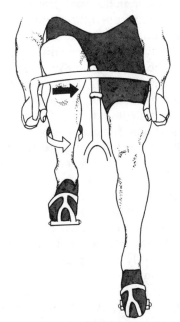

Figure 13 Inward pivoting of the shank produced by pronation. (Excessive pronation will also tend to produce an unnatural abduction of the knee joint, represented by the black arrow.)

the system, and serious injuries can result. The mechanisms can be investigated with the four-link model.

If we do not restrict the range of motion of the subtalar joint of the model, then the extent of eversion can greatly exceed 10° when the foot is loaded during pedaling. When the bottom surface of the foot link is constrained to move with the top surface of the pedal, the shank will be internally rotated beyond the limits of tolerance of the system. Adduction of the thigh at the hip joint can only partially compensate for internal rotation of the shank, and so undesirable mechanical stresses are exerted upon the model.

The stresses will tend to abduct the knee joint, as shown in Figure 13. Furthermore, these stresses will be greatest when the forces causing knee extension are greatest. Recall that the knee is not designed to allow abduction, and so abnormal stresses will occur at the sides of the joint. Specifically, the side of the joint nearest the frame of the bicycle will be stretched, and the outer side of the knee joint will be compressed. The uneven pressure distribution on the joint surfaces might well produce some of the nagging injuries that are frequently diagnosed by the nonspecialist as "cyclist's knee."

Another undesirable effect of excessive pronation is abnormal stress upon the pulley mechanism of the knee caused by the unnatural abduction of the knee. Tension in the quadriceps tendon caused by forceful contraction of the quadriceps muscle group will tend to pull the mechanism toward the outer side of the knee. Thus the patella, which normally glides smoothly in the groove of the femur, begins to exert compressive forces on the outer side of the groove. Eventually the bony surfaces and the covering of cartilage can become damaged; this can lead to a variety of painful disorders that are described by such names as "excessive lateral pressure syndrome," "chondromalacia patella," and "synovitis." In addition, the abnormal stresses on the system can also cause the cyclist's pelvis to be tilted forward to produce a swayback condition of the lower spine. The condition can result in nagging backache for many riders. However, the present model will not allow us to explore the mechanics involved.

Clearly, excessive pronation is most undesirable. However, it has been reported that a combination of poor posture and gait, together with excessive standing and inadequate footwear has resulted in pronation problems for a fairly large percentage of the population in modern society. Some individuals are apparently born with a congenital predisposition for foot disorders, but anyone can take precautions to avoid mechanical changes that will produce excessive pronation. It is first essential to understand the process by which a previously healthy foot degenerates so that it cannot maintain rigidity when it is being used as a link mechanism.

A mechanically efficient foot can approximate rigidity when three structural mechanisms combine to "lock" the various joints so that the foot forms a weight-bearing arch. The three mechanisms are associated with the bones, the ligaments, and the muscles, respectively.

The bones of the mechanically sound foot are architecturally compatible with one another like the separate building blocks of a masonry window frame. A force exerted on the top of either of these structures will be transmitted to the points of support of the arch, and the load will also tend to hold the components firmly against one another. Natural stone is immensely strong when it is compressed by a sustained load, but our bones are constructed from dynamic, living tissues that change shape in response to long-term stress. Therefore, unless the bones of our feet receive mechanical support from other structures, they will gradually lose their desirable shapes and the arch of the foot will slowly flatten. This condition has been referred to as flatfeet or fallen arches and is characterized by a flattening of the longitudinal arch of the foot. Although a foot that has a flattened longitudinal arch may not produce undesirable changes in structure or function, the condition can frequently be associated with the inability of the foot to function as a mechanically sound rigid link.

The second structural mechanism that assists the foot to function as a rigid link is composed of the various ligaments that attach bones to one another. In the mechanically sound foot the ligaments become taut when adjacent bones pivot to the desirable limits of their ranges of motion. The ligaments will then prevent excessive motion and protect the bones from stress. If the desirable range of motion of a joint is exceeded, sensitive nerve endings in the ligaments transmit pain impulses that warn the body about the danger of physical damage. In particular, a large, flat ligament under the skin of the sole of the foot known as the plantar ligament helps to preserve the arch of the foot and can be likened to that of a bowstring, which maintains the curvature of an archery bow. The strong fibrous tissue from which all ligaments are constructed will withstand relatively large tension forces, but if the forces become excessive and sustained the ligaments will stretch. Ligaments that have been slightly stretched appear to have sufficient elasticity to allow them to passively contract back to their original lengths during rest. However, repeated, sustained stress can permanently stretch a ligament so that it will permit an excessive range of motion of the joint that it was previously protecting. Continued stress will then deform the bones on either side of the joint.

The third mechanism that helps to maintain the arch is the muscular system of the foot. Numerous small, intrinsic muscles within the foot itself help to support parts of the complex structure. In addition, the arch is maintained by two important muscles that have their origins on the shank. The most important of these (the tibialis posterior muscle) lies underneath the calf muscles and is attached by its tendon to the undersurface of the highest point of the arch. The other muscle (tibialis anterior) was mentioned earlier as the major dorsiflexor of the foot, but it also has a secondary function of elevating the arch during dorsiflexion. These muscles are particularly important when an individual stands still for long periods of time because the small muscles within the foot are relatively nonfunctional during inactivity. When the mechanically efficient foot is active, many of the muscles are in a permanent state of partial contraction known as "tonus," so that some muscular mechanism is always helping to maintain good arch mechanics. However, muscle tonus is lost if muscles are not exercised, so that the deconditioned individual places increased stress on the bones and ligaments.

In summary, the muscles provide a "first line of defense" against undesirable changes in the structure and function of the foot. If the strength of the muscles that support the arch of the foot is maintained, relatively little stress will be placed on the other structures during a vigorous activity such as cycling. However, if muscle tonus is lost, excessive stress will be placed on the ligaments. If the stress is sustained for a period of time then the ligaments will stretch, a condition known as ligamentous laxity. Continued stress will then create undesirable compression in some areas of contact between bones, and the bones will eventually deform so that the foot can no longer function as a rigid link. Eventually the foot will become structurally pronated, and the degree of pronation will progressively worsen when continued loads are applied to the foot.

In addition to a loss of muscle tonus, a number of other factors can contribute to the deterioration of arch mechanics. The most important is probably genetics. For example, an individual who has inherited a tendency for flatfeet is much more prone to foot problems than someone who has more desirable foot structure. Unfortunately, we have no control over our genetic makeup, and therefore some individuals must take particularly good care of their feet if they hope to avoid injuries. Another important factor that can adversely affect arch mechanics is unsuitable shoes. A well fitting cycling shoe that has a rigid sole can effectively act as a splint that holds the foot in a desirable position. However, cycling shoes and many other types of everyday footwear may restrict the motions of the foot to such an extent that the foot can become excessively rigid at all times. When this occurs, the foot functions well as a rigid link, but it lacks the ability to absorb shock during walking and running. This condition has been called the "solid sole shoe syndrome," and it can lead to injuries when the cyclist is engaging in vigorous activities other than cycling.

Another factor that contributes to deterioration of the arches is excessive fatigue. Muscles lose their ability to exert maximum force as they become fatigued, and so the rider who appears to have good foot mechanics may develop mechanical deficiencies after a long, hard ride. This fact indicates that the cyclist should follow a training program that will gradually improve the strength and endurance of intrinsic and extrinsic muscles of the foot as mileage is gradually increased.

If you have obvious weaknesses in these muscles you can use specific exercises to strengthen them. Try these two simple procedures. Spread a towel flat on the floor, and sit on a chair with your bare feet on the near edge of the towel. Keep your heels on the floor and use your toes to gradually pull the towel toward you, an inch at a time. Each time you pull the towel you will forcibly contract the intrinsic muscles of the foot.

The extrinsic muscles can be strengthened in the following manner. Sit with your fists between your knees, as shown in Figure 14. Keep your heels on the floor and squeeze your knees together against your fists. At the same time, press your toes together as hard as you can. You will know that you are performing the exercise correctly when

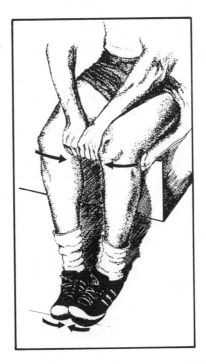

Figure 14 Strengthening exercise for the extrinsic muscles of the feet, devised by Dr. Klein of the University of Texas.

your arches tend to rise up from the floor. Exercises such as these, and any others that may be prescribed by a competent specialist, can be performed whenever you are watching television or reading.

A training program that is designed to gradually increase the intensity, frequency, and duration of cycling mileage, together with specific flexibility and strengthening exercises and a sensible choice of footwear, will help the healthy cyclist to maintain good arch mechanics. Unfortunately, many active riders have already undergone structural changes that make excessive pronation inevitable. These cyclists must seek help if they are to avoid becoming injured as the result of their mechanical shortcomings. One successful method is to reorient the foot within the cycling shoe by means of an in-shoe orthotic. Although rare individuals may be able to use off-the-shelf arch supports, the function of an orthotic is to control the extent of pronation by accurately positioning the forefoot and the rearfoot with respect to one another and limiting the range of motion of each segment of the foot so that they can interact to maintain a functional arch. The precise orientation of each segment can only be determined by careful measurements made by a qualified specialist. A comfortable, effective orthotic must be manufactured precisely to the needs of the individual cyclist.

Experience has shown that a rigid-soled cycling shoe provides a better base of support for an orthotic than a flexible shoe. For this reason the touring cyclist who is fitted with orthotics should probably avoid flexible footwear and use a rigid-soled cycling shoe. Furthermore, because the cyclist is not subjected to impacts on the feet, a rigid orthotic appears to provide comfortable and effective control in most cases. A thin, rigid orthotic will also occupy a smaller volume of the shoe than the more substantial flexible type. It is particularly important that the orthotic does not elevate the heel out of the shoe because this increases the danger of the cyclist's foot being pulled out of the shoe in a sprinting or hill-climbing situation. Naturally, new shoes should be tried with the orthotics in place.

The effects of custom-made orthotics are illustrated in Figure 15. The subject is a world-class rider who previously pronated so badly that he repeatedly struck the inner side of the ankles against his cranks when he exerted maximum forces against the pedals in a sprint. The orthotic positioned his foot so that pronation was markedly reduced. Consequently, the amount of inward rotation of the shank was reduced and the hip joint no longer had to adduct to compensate for excessive inward rotation. As a result the side-to-side motion of the knee almost disappeared.

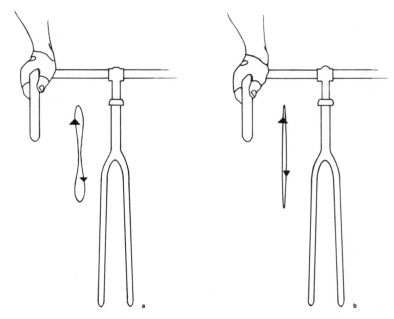

Figure 15(a) Path of the knee without orthotics

Figure 15(b) Path of the knee with orthotics

Note that many cyclists exhibit the side-to-side motion of the knee, known as "wobbly knee," but that this ungainly pattern is not in itself indicative of a serious problem. In fact, if adduction of the thigh can compensate for the inward rotation caused by the tilt of the ankle joint, the rider may never have problems. However, it must be stressed that if the motion is caused by excessive pronation the effects will probably worsen with time, so early treatment is advisable.

Malalignments of the Forefoot and Rearfoot.   As described earlier, the desirable foot (or neutral foot) is characterized by having both the flat base of the heel bone and the flat plane formed by the metatarsal heads perpendicular to the long axis of the shank (see Figure 12). However, only a few fortunate individuals may possess this desirable foot structure. Malalignments of the front part of the foot (the forefoot) and the rear part of the foot (the rearfoot) are extremely common. Consequently, many cyclists have mechanical deficiencies that can contribute to injuries if compensations are not made to accommodate the anatomical structures involved.

Figure 16 shows four distinct malalignments that have been recognized in the general population. A cyclist may have any one of these conditions to a greater or lesser extent, but in some cases an individual may have a complex combination (of either 16a and 16d or 16b and 16c) present in the same foot. Precise clinical diagnosis should be made on an individual basis by an orthopedic surgeon, a podiatrist, or some other qualified professional.

Forefoot varus, an extremely common condition, is characterized by forefoot inversion while the rearfoot is aligned like that of the neutral foot. Conversely, *forefoot valgus,* which is much less common, is characterized by forefoot eversion while the rearfoot is aligned like that of the neutral foot. *Rearfoot varus* is characterized by inversion of the rearfoot, while *rearfoot valgus* is characterized by eversion of the rearfoot.

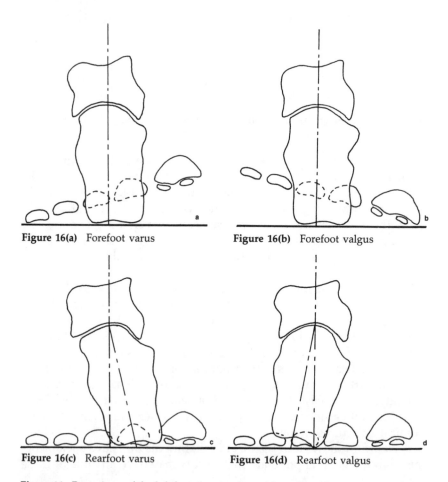

Figure 16(a)   Forefoot varus   **Figure 16(b)**   Forefoot valgus

Figure 16(c)   Rearfoot varus   **Figure 16(d)**   Rearfoot valgus

Figure 16   Rear views of the left foot showing the ankle and heel bones and the bones of the ball of the foot

Using the Model to Examine
the Effects of Malalignments of the Foot

Forefoot varus: If we twist the foot link on the model so that the forefoot is inverted a few degrees with respect to the rearfoot and we then permit a few degrees of frictionless inversion and eversion on either side of this position, we can simulate a forefoot varus condition. When the flat base of the forefoot is attached to the top surface of a bicycle pedal the whole of the model will tend to rotate toward the bicycle frame in order to bring the two flat surfaces together. However, we have previously stipulated that the hip joint must remain in a fixed location (which is determined by the position of the seat in the living rider). In order to compensate for the malalignment the foot must evert, as shown in Figure 17. Provided that the extent of malalignment is less than or equal to the few degrees of available eversion, the model can now exert forces on the pedal without being subjected to additional stress.

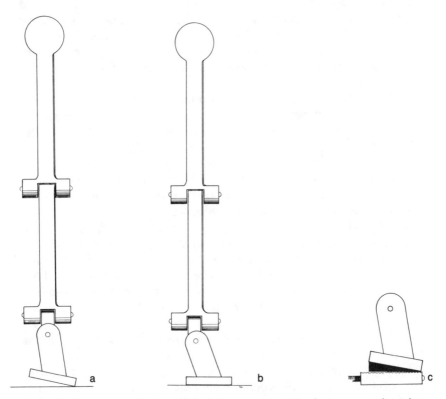

Figure 17 Front view of the three-dimensional model: (a) forefoot varus condition before eversion; (b) eversion compensates for the condition; (c) correction using a wedge

If we now assume that the extent of the malalignment is greater than the available range of eversion, then damaging stress will be placed on the model. Clearly, the hip joint will be protected from stress if it can be adducted sufficiently; however, the knee joint will tend to be forced into abduction. This latter motion is not compatible with the structure of the joint, and it will tend to stretch the inner side of the joint and compress the outer side of the joint. In addition, the pulley mechanism of the knee joint will be forced to the outer side, as described in the section dealing with excessive pronation. Predictably, a rider who has a significant forefoot varus condition will suffer the kinds of knee injuries that are associated with excessive pronation.

The model would evidently also be subjected to forces that would tend to stretch the inner side and compress the outer side of the ankle joint. However, ankle injuries appear to be relatively rare in cycling, and so it is assumed that this joint has sufficient strength and resilience to withstand these stresses.

As was described earlier, a mild forefoot varus can be accommodated with slight eversion. However, a foot that is repeatedly loaded in an everted position probably will begin to undergo structural changes, especially if the muscles cannot provide the support necessary to maintain good arch mechanics. Therefore, a danger exists of the condition becoming progressively worse as the result of a demanding training program.

We can now use the model to examine possible ways of compensating for a forefoot varus condition. A wedge whose angle corresponds to the malalignment of the forefoot varus can be inserted between the forefoot and the pedal (Figure 17c), and the model can now perform with no damaging stress to the system. In reality this can be accomplished in one of two ways. The first and least expensive is to construct a wedge on the top surface of the pedal itself. However, because a cycling shoe has a rigid sole, the wedge will invert the whole foot. A long-term effect of cycling in this position could possibly be to stretch the lateral ligamentous structure of the ankle joint. The cyclist may then be prone to inversion sprains while walking and running. Another alternative would be to build the wedge under the forefoot area of the inside of the shoe. Although this would be a more expensive solution it would permit the rearfoot to remain in neutral alignment with the shank.

Unfortunately, both of these corrections are short-term solutions that treat the effect of an anatomical problem, rather than long-term solutions that treat the cause of the problem. Prolonged cycling with any forefoot wedge will progressively flatten the arch mechanism of the foot, and the temporary relief provided by the wedge may actually mask an ongoing deterioration of the structure of the foot. The most successful long-term solution to the problem will probably be to re-orient the alignment of the structures of the foot with an orthotic device.

Forefoot valgus: If we twist the foot link so that the "forefoot" is everted a few degrees with respect to the "rearfoot" and we also permit a few degrees of frictionless inversion and eversion either side of this position, we can simulate a forefoot valgus position. When the foot link is placed flat on a pedal the model has a tendency to rotate away from the bicycle frame (see Figure 18). If the amount of malalignment is less than or equal to the amount of available inversion, then the model can apply pedaling force without undue stress on the model. However, if the malalignment is greater than the available inversion, the tendency will be to stretch the outer side of the knee joint and to compress the inner side of the knee joint. The pulley system of the knee would also be displaced toward the inner side of the knee. This condition is relatively rare among cyclists, but it will probably produce characteristic knee injuries if appropriate compensations are not made. Corrections for forefoot valgus are comparable with those recommended for forefoot varus. A wedge either on the pedal or the inside of the shoe can provide a temporary relief from symptoms, but the long-term effects should be discussed with a competent specialist.

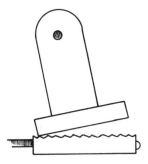

Figure 18(a)   Forefoot valgus condition

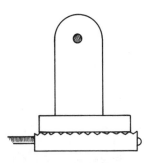

Figure 18(b)   Excessive inversion without correction

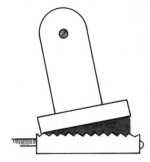

Figure 18(c)   Correction using a wedge mounted on the pedal

Rearfoot varus and rearfoot valgus: In both of these conditions the "forefoot" of the model can be attached to a bicycle pedal, and the model can apply pedaling force to the pedal without any undue short-term stress upon the model. Unfortunately, however, rearfoot mal-alignments place stresses upon the structures of the foot during other everyday activities such as walking and running. The undesirable stresses produce compensations that may eventually effect the dynamics of the forefoot. Therefore, although rearfoot malalignments may not produce immediate injuries to the cyclist, it is advisable to seek advice from a specialist if long-term problems are to be avoided.

Malalignment of the Knees.   In the mechanically sound individual the knee joints are aligned vertically above the ankle joints during comfortable stance. Similarly, the hip joints tend to be aligned vertically above the knee joints. However, many females and some males who have wide hips have a knock-kneed appearance due to the convergence of the thighs at the knee joints. Conversely, some individuals have a bowlegged appearance due to the fact that the knee joints are aligned outside of the vertical line joining the hip and ankle joints. These malalignments may either be inherited traits or the results of illness or disease (see Figure 19).

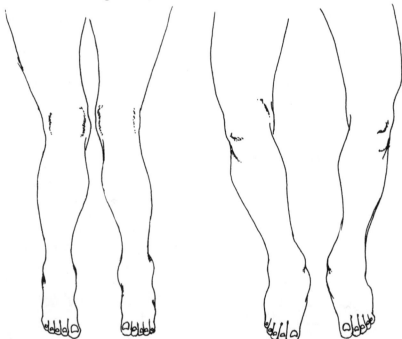

Figure 19(a) Knock-knees   **Figure 19(b)** Bowlegs

An examination of the population of active cyclists reveals that some individuals have enjoyed many years of injury free cycling even though they have pronounced malalignment of the knees, while less fortunate individuals have suffered discomfort or injury as the result of comparable malalignments. Some of the former individuals may have avoided injury by limiting the intensity, duration, and frequency of their cycling activity, but undoubtedly some very active, injury free riders have malalignments. The model may be used to illustrate factors that contribute to injury free mechanics and to examine those factors that predispose a cyclist to injury from malalignments.

The fortunate cyclist who has the hip, knee, and ankle joints in continuous alignment may be represented by the two-dimensional model in which the segments lie in a single plane and the three joint axes are all perpendicular to that plane. Consequently, muscle forces exerted in that plane will flex and extend the segments as described earlier. However, the three-dimensional model will be necessary to examine the mechanical effects of malalignments of the knees.

Bowlegs: If the links that correspond to the thigh and shank are bent in two places so that the hip and knee axes remain parallel to the axis of the ankle, the model retains many of the characteristics of the two-dimensional model (see Figure 20a). The most important difference is that muscle forces acting at the knee joint are exerted obliquely instead of in the plane of the thigh and shank links. For the injury free condition it must be assumed that the structure of the joint is sufficiently resilient to withstand the compression forces that will be placed on the inner side of the joint by both the knee flexors and the knee extensors. Perhaps this may also be aided by an increase in the strength of the knee flexor on the outer side of the rear of the thigh (the lateral hamstring) and the knee extensor on the outer side of the front of the thigh (the vastus lateralis).

A number of possible adaptations of the model illustrate the factors that can produce injury as the result of bowlegs. In the situation described above, it is readily apparent that the application of oblique forces across the knee joint can compress the medial side of the joint to an extent that will produce damage. In addition, the force of contraction of the quadriceps would tend to pull the patella to the inner side so that it would no longer be tracking as part of the pulley mechanism. Possible effects of this were described earlier.

The model can also be adapted so that the links corresponding to the thigh and shank are bent so that the axis of the knee joint is no longer parallel to the axes of the hip and ankle joints (see Figure 20b). Muscle forces across the knee joint will now be directed obliquely, and the model may now be subjected to compression on the medial side. In addition, when the hip is flexed the shank must pivot around the

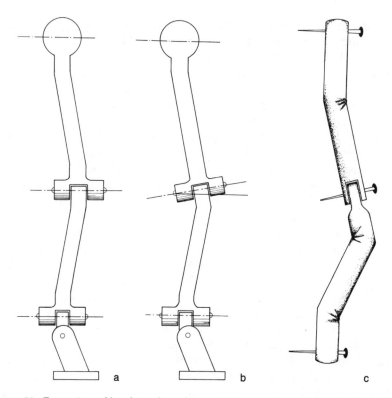

Figure 20 Front view of bowlegged conditions: (a) knee axis parallel to the hip and ankle axes; (b) knee axis not parallel to the hip and ankle axes; (c) mechanical model constructed from drinking straws and pins

knee axis to cause simultaneous flexion and outward rotation. You can observe this three-dimensional motion if you construct an actual mechanical model using two drinking straws to represent the thigh and shank links and three pins to represent the joint axes (see Figure 20c). If the foot is not constrained by a toe clip and cleat, the foot will pivot outward during knee flexion and will pivot inward durng knee extension. This may have no adverse effects on the cyclist. The addition of a toe clip and cleat will lock the foot and prevent outward rotation of the shank. In this case knee flexion will force an unnatural inward rotation of the shank at the knee joint. Similarly, knee extension will force an unnatural outward rotation of the knee joint. The results of these stresses will probably produce undesirable pressures on the joint surfaces and some degree of ligamentous laxity.

Finally, the model may be modified with the links corresponding to the thigh and shank bent so that the ankle axis is no longer parallel to the other two axes. In this situation the only way that the foot link can rest on the pedal is by everting the forefoot link. Even if the extent of the eversion is within the range of motion allowed by the joint, the model will still be subjected to stresses in the joints of the system. The cyclist who is subjected to comparable stresses for an extended period of time will probably undergo compensatory changes in the structure of the foot. In effect, the continuous loading of the inner side of the foot during both walking and cycling will tend to pronate the foot. The progressive, undesirable effects of pronation were discussed earlier. Once again, an orthotic device in the shoe can often realign the foot and, in many cases, successfully reduce the extent of malalignment of the knees.

Knock-knees: As was the case with bowlegs, a cyclist conceivably could have the axes of the hip, knee, and ankle parallel to one another, despite a marked malalignment. In this case the muscle forces across the knee joint would be exerted obliquely, so that the outer side of the joint would be compressed and the pulley mechanism of the knee would tend to be forced away from the midline of the body. However, if the medial vastus muscle is strengthened with appropriate exercises, it will tend to counteract this undesirable situation by pulling the kneecap back toward the inner side of the knee joint. If the anatomical structures of the knee are resilient enough to withstand these oblique forces, the cyclist may be able to cycle without discomfort or injury. However, if the mechanical tolerance of the knee is exceeded, injuries will be inevitable. If the model is adapted so that the thigh and shank links are bent the knee axis will no longer be parallel to the axes of the hip and ankle. In this case hip flexion will produce simultaneous knee flexion and inward rotation of the shank. Once again, this can be demonstrated with a mechanical model constructed from two drinking straws and three pins.

Abnormal Angle of Gait.   If you walk comfortably along a straight line on either a wet surface or a sand beach you will leave a series of footprints that can be used to estimate your angle of gait. Most individuals walk with a slight toe-out gait so that a line drawn along the midline of the footprint forms an angle of between 5° and 10° with the direction of travel (see Figure 21). Although undoubtedly some injury free cyclists have abnormal gait angles, any significant differences in the form of obvious toe-in gait or excessive toe-out gait will usually predispose a cyclist to injuries. These problems can be examined with the three-dimensional model.

The injury free toe-in condition can be simulated by twisting the ankle bone link to form a toe-in position of the foot. Provided that the hip, knee, and ankle axes remain parallel, the foot can be attached to the top of a pedal so that it can exert pedaling forces without producing

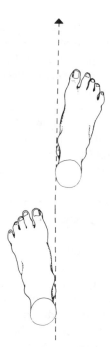

Figure 21   Foot placement for typical angle of gait

undue stresses on the model. The important factor is, of course, that the cleat and toe clip must be adjusted to conform with the toe-in position of the foot. If the cleat and toe clip are adjusted to fit a normal angle of gait, the toe-in model will be forcibly twisted outward during pedaling. Stress will be placed on all of the joints, but in view of the restrictive anatomy of the knee joint, the twisting would probably distort the pulley mechanism formed by the kneecap and the femur. Contraction of the quadriceps muscle group would tend to produce uneven pressures between the kneecap and the femur; the injurious effects of these malalignments have been discussed earlier.

Similarly, it may be obvious that if the ankle bone link is twisted in the opposite direction to form an excessive toe-out position, the model can perform without undue stress provided that the foot link is attached to the pedal in the toe-out position. Any attempt to realign the foot in a normal angle of gait will twist the model inward. Probably, this undesirable procedure would also adversely affect the knees of the cyclist. The three-dimensional model can now be used to examine the effects of conditions in which the tibia is twisted along its length so that the ankle and foot are rotated either inward or outward. Either of these conditions are referred to as tibial torsion.

If the axes of the hip and knee joints are allowed to remain parallel and the shank link of the model is twisted to produce outward rotation of the ankle and foot, the axis of the ankle joint will be rotated to some new position, as shown in Figure 22. As a first step to understanding the mechanics of this arrangement, notice that the foot link is positioned outside of the plane formed by the thigh and shank links when the foot link forms a right angle with the shank. But, if the foot link is pivoted so that it forms a straight line with the shank link (plantar flexed), it moves back into the plane of the thigh and shank. Therefore, when the model is placed on a bicycle with the foot link resting on a pedal and forming a right angle with the shank, the foot will naturally be turned to the outside. Provided that the foot is *not* restrained with a cleat and toe clip and the subtalar joint is in a neutral position, the model can now produce a pedaling action that does not place excessive stress on the system. However, the foot will pivot freely on the pedal so that the rear part of the foot moves away from the bicycle frame as the ankle joint begins to plantar flex. At the same time the subtalar joint will be forced to evert in order to keep the foot link flat on the pedal. Subsequently, when the ankle is dorsiflexed, the rear part of the foot will pivot freely back toward the bicycle frame, and the subtalar joint will return to the neutral position when the ankle is dorsiflexed. Of course, the range of motion of the ankle joint during cycling is considerably less than the 90° range described above (see Figure 6), so that the foot will pivot to a lesser extent than indicated in Figure 22. Provided that the hip joint will permit sufficient internal and external rotation without placing excessive stress on the knees, the cyclist with external tibial torsion may remain injury free despite the rather ungainly appearance of the motion involved.

If the same model is now restrained by a cleat and toe clip with the ankle joint at 90° and the foot link in the turned-out position, the foot will be unable to pivot freely on the pedal surface. Therefore, when the foot is plantar flexed the rear part of the foot will be prevented from pivoting away from the bicycle frame and so the shank will be forced inward toward the bicycle frame, and the subtalar joint will be forcibly inverted. Unfortunately, however, the position of the hip joint must remain fixed, and so the model is forced into an undesirable knock-kneed position while the ankle joint is plantar flexed. If the extent of this distortion exceeds the limits of resilience of the system, the stress will produce compression on the lateral side of the knee, and the pulley mechanism of the knee will be forced toward the outside of the knee joint.

If the cyclist attempts to overcome the undesirable effects of this situation by moving the cleat and toe clip to align the foot parallel with

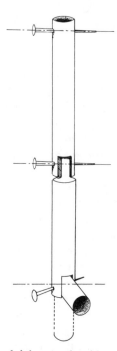

Figure 22   Tibial torsion of the left leg simulated by a mechanical model constructed from drinking straws and pins

the bicycle frame, other problems will likely be encountered. If the model representing an external tibial torsion condition is attached to a bicycle pedal with the foot link parallel to the bicycle frame and with the knee joint fully extended, the hip joint will permit internal rotation of the shank and the thigh. However, when the knee and hip are flexed in a cycling position, the internal rotation will be restricted to the shank link. This in turn will place an undesirable stress on the knee joint while the model is stationary. Furthermore, when the model produces a pedaling action the malalignment of the contacting surfaces of the knee joint will tend to further stress the joint. If these stresses exceed the limits of tolerance of the system, continued cycling will progressively damage the components.

It should be readily apparent that a cyclist who has an internal tibial torsion condition may also be able to function injury free if the foot is not restrained with a cleat and toe clip. However, the same individual may be subjected to undesirable stresses when the foot is attached to the pedal.

Although some individuals cannot resolve these kinds of mechanical problems with conventional bicycle components, many cyclists who have mild tibial torsion can function without exceeding the limits of mechanical tolerance if they carefully adjust the positions of cleats and toe clips so that stresses on the knees are minimized. Many individuals have successfully utilized an ingenious commercial device (The Fit Kit), which aligns the functional axis of the ankle/subtalar complex with the axis of the pedal. In addition, a promising alternative to the conventional pedal (The Biopedal) permits adjustments to foot position as well as some pivoting of the foot during cycling.

In summary, the three-dimensional model can be used to demonstrate that pathomechanical conditions of excessive pronation, malalignments of the forefoot and rearfoot, malalignments of the knees, and abnormal angle of gait will predispose a cyclist to injury. The susceptibility of the individual to specific injuries is clearly determined by the severity of his or her pathomechanical condition, and the likelihood of injury increases with increases in the intensity of cycling and the weekly mileage.

All of the conditions discussed so far have been examined for cycling in a seated position. You should also be aware that additional problems are associated with riding while standing up in the pedals. In particular, potential problems are associated with fully extending the knee joints during either sprinting or hill climbing. Because this technique is highly inefficient, it is unlikely that any skilled rider would ever fully extend the knees, but anyone coaching novices should be aware of the mechanics involved.

You may recall that the last few degrees of knee extension are accompanied by external rotation of the shank; this mechanism "locks" and stabilizes the knee joint. Simultaneously, if the shank exerts a large pedaling force on the foot, the foot tends to pronate, as described earlier. The pronation will, in turn, produce internal rotation of the shank. If the rigid shank link of the three-dimensional model is subjected to simultaneous internal rotation and external rotation, it will provide immovable resistance to both the ankle and knee joints. In other words, the continued stress will eventually damage one of the joints. Because of the vulnerability of the human knee joint, this structure will likely sustain injury under these conditions. The important point to recognize in this situation is that an otherwise injury free cyclist who is just within the tolerance limits of the knee joint as the result of moderate pronation during seated cycling will suddenly be subjected to additional stress on the knee due to the extra few degrees of rotation provided by the locking mechanism. The added rotational stress produced by full knee extension may now produce injury by forcing the knee beyond its tolerance limits.

Where Do You Go From Here?

Cycling offers us a vigorous and enjoyable form of transportation and recreation, and perhaps an opportunity to compete in one of the most popular sports in the world. This unique activity can also be a lifelong pastime for those who are fortunate enough to enjoy robust health. It is unfortunate when an enthusiastic cyclist must give up the activity as the result of a serious injury, especially if the injury was preventable. The biomechanical modeling technique used in this chapter can be used to help you to understand the causes of many pathomechanical injuries. In addition, the technique can help you to explore the possible means of preventing these injuries.

Finally, it is appropriate to regard the human body as being in a state of dynamic unstable equilibrium. In other words, you must constantly work at maintaining the range of motion at each of the joints and the appropriate strength of the muscles that move the complex linkage mechanism that makes up the body. If some part of the mechanism begins to function inefficiently, inevitably compensations will continue to produce further undesirable changes. You can maintain your body in precisely the same way that you maintain your bicycle. Do not wait until something is beyond repair before you try to fix it, and look carefully for signs of wear and tear due to malalignments. Finally, if you do not understand why something is not working the way it should be, seek the advice of an expert.

Suggested Readings

Hlavac, H.F. (1979). *The foot book*. Mountain View, CA: World Publications.

Leadbetter, W.B., & Schneider, M.J. (1982). Orthopedics. In P. Harris, J. van der Reis Krausz, & V. van der Reis Krausz, *The bicycling book: Transportation, recreation, and sport*. New York: The Dial Press.

CHAPTER 9

Medical Aspects of Racing

Blake Powell, MD
Medical Consultant for the U.S. Cycling Team

The medical concerns of the cycle racer are unusual, particularly because of cycling's prolonged activity. For example, the 1983 Professional World Cycling Championships, won by Greg LeMond, covered 270 km (167.4 mi) in 7 hr, 1 min, and 21 s. Such long and continuous periods of activity put the rider at risk for overuse injuries, dehydration, fatigue, and environmental problems. In addition, cycle racing is a sport of speed that offers little protection to the participant. Greg LeMond averaged 38.45 kph (23.84 mph) on that championship ride, a figure that does not convey a true sense of the top speeds that are often achieved in racing, particularly going downhill.

High speeds with little protection and prolonged activity with prolonged exposure can combine synergistically to give the rider significant medical problems. Everyone involved with cycle racing needs a sound knowledge of such problems in order to prevent problems or to correct them if they occur. The medical aspects of cycle racing can be divided into five areas: injuries, environmental problems, medical problems, general problems, and nutrition/drugs.

Injuries

A survey of cycling injuries in the medical literature since 1968 reveals few articles that focus on injuries specific to cycle racing. One of the fortunate reasons for this paucity of information is that cycle-racing injuries are few in number and types. Such injuries as do occur can be divided into the two major categories of impact injuries and overuse injuries.

Impact Injuries

Impact injuries are caused by crashing, accidents that can occur at any time, particularly among less-experienced riders. Tactical errors and lack of knowledge about how to reflexively react to acute situations contribute to accidents in the less-experienced ranks. Fatigue also plays a part. As riders become tired during a race, reflexes slow, and more accidents tend to occur. Once again, this can particularly apply to the less-experienced and often less well-trained rider who becomes fatigued quickly.

The extent of injuries in crashes is basically dependent on two things—the experience of the rider and whether a motor vehicle is involved. Experienced riders know how to fall. They "bunch up." They pull in their elbows and duck their heads, essentially landing on their shoulders, hips, and backs. As a result, injuries are usually reduced in severity. On the other hand, if a motor vehicle is involved in a cycle accident, the rider often suffers serious injury. Multiple trauma (injury to numerous body systems) is common. Most of the approximately 1,000 cycling deaths that occur in the United States each year are due to cyclist/motor-vehicle interactions, and perhaps 80% or more of those deaths are due to major head trauma.

A crash requires some precrash preparation. Support personnel must work systematically. First, the cycles must be removed from the injured cyclists (after release of the pedal straps). Second, the victims and cycles must be carefully moved off the racecourse. If a rider has an obvious deformity, especially of the neck, such movement must be done by qualified personnel. Third, the riders should be carefully examined, and the examination must include removal of clothing. Usually the responses to a crash are thoughtless, willy-nilly reactions. The victims deserve better.

Abrasions.   Abrasions are the most common impact injuries incurred in cycle racing. Usually affecting the left side of the body because both criterium and track racing are done in counterclockwise fashion, these lesions are scrapes. The top layer of the skin is removed, and watertight integrity is lost. Often particles of asphalt and dirt are embedded in the area, resulting in a contaminated wound ripe for infection.

Treatment consists of an initial careful cleaning. At home a rider can use a deodorant soap and a washcloth, taking care to remove all of the dirt and asphalt. Removing the asphalt is particularly important because, if some remains, the area can become permanently tatooed. Such a cleaning is a painful process. Indeed, these wounds are probably the most painful of all of the injuries that occur in cycling. Extensive abrasions can be pretreated at a medical facility with a local anesthetic such as viscous Xylocaine before scrubbing in order to help the rider.

After a careful cleaning, the area can be covered with an antibiotic spray or ointment. Healing of such wounds takes time, and until they have healed sufficiently to become watertight again, they are at risk for infection, and so adequate precautions against contamination must be used. During the healing period a rider may use one of the many anesthetic or painkilling sprays on the market in order to be comfortable (especially while sleeping).

Contusions.   Contusions are bruises. When an area of the body sustains a blow, many capillaries in the impact area are damaged. Blood leaks out into the surrounding tissues. Swelling occurs. The area becomes tender and eventually discolors as the released blood nears the skin surface. Contusions need ice. It should be placed in a plastic bag and the bag put directly on the skin and left there for 15 to 20 min. This treatment should be repeated 4 to 6 times a day for the first 2 to 3 days. After that heat can be used.

Ice is necessary to help prevent swelling by keeping damaged capillaries constricted and reducing the metabolic activity of the inflammatory cells in the area. A rider should remember that abrasions are usually associated with contusions and treat the areas with ice.

Lacerations.   Lacerations are cuts of the skin. Those that are extensive or are deep enough to allow the wound to gape open must be sutured. If not, the injury will leave a larger scar and is at greater risk for infection.

Strains and Sprains.   A strain is damage to a muscle and/or a tendon, whereas a sprain is damage to a ligament. Both injuries are categorized by degrees of severity: first degree, microtears; second degree, partial tears; third degree, complete tears. Because the cycle supports the cyclist, racers usually sustain few strains and sprains, except perhaps in an unusually violent crash in which the rider is thrown around a great deal. Swelling, pain, and decreased function of a joint or limb are the characteristics of such injuries. Once again, ice is the hallmark of treatment. A rider can remember the acronym

R.I.C.E.—Rest, Ice, Compression, Elevation.

Rest the affected area. Use ice as previously described. Apply compression to the injury through the use of an elastic wrap. Elevate the area to at least the level of the heart. Some people add R to the end of the acronym to make R.I.C.E.R., the second R standing for rehabilitation. Any injured body part must be slowly brought back to full use. Many injured riders are impatient to resume their former exercise programs, but an injury must be rehabilitated slowly or a chronic problem can result.

Fractures/Separations/Dislocations. In cycle racing, the two most common fractures are those of the ribs and the clavicle (collarbone). Less common are upper extremity (arm) fractures such as forearm or finger breaks, or lower extremity (leg) problems such as patella (kneecap) or femur (upper leg) injuries. As a matter of fact, the Medical Director for the United States Cycling Federation, Thomas Dickson, M.D., states that he has never seen a lower-extremity fracture and rarely an arm one, but they can happen.

Usually fractures of either the ribs or the clavicle are uncomplicated. Unfortunately, a bad rib injury can cause a pneumothorax (collapsed lung) with its attendant problems of shortness of breath and possibly a serious tension pneumothorax. Any rider involved in a crash should be carefully examined. If the cyclist is short of breath and is having rib pain, or if obvious deformities are present anywhere, he or she must receive further medical evaluation, including x-ray.

Closely associated with clavicle fractures are shoulder separations, injuries to the joint between the end of the clavicle and the scapula (shoulder blade). These are also fairly common in cycle racing. Such injuries can be of increasing degrees of severity, from a mild sprain of the ligaments in the area to complete disruption of them. Pain and/or deformity on the top of the shoulder suggests a separation, and the rider should seek further medical help. Finally, joint dislocations can possibly occur in a crash, usually to the upper extremity. Once again, any significant pain and/or deformity should make the rider seek assistance.

Head Injury. Head injuries, common occurrences in cycle racing, can cause concussions. A rider has had a concussion if he or she received a blow to the head that caused loss of consciousness and amnesia of the events surrounding the incident. Some experts state that a period of mental disorientation after a head injury, without associated unconsciousness, constitutes a mild concussion. A rider who sustains any degree of concussion or major head trauma must be carefully examined, x-rayed if indicated, and observed for a period of time. The rider must not be allowed to get back on the cycle and resume riding.

As stated earlier, the deaths associated with cycling are mainly the result of significant head injury. Unfortunately, most cycle racers still wear the traditional "hair net" leather helmet, which offers little protection. Hard-shell helmets lined with high-density foam give the rider much more head protection in an impact. If the hard helmet continues to gain popularity for both training (few riders train with helmets) and racing, the sequelae of head trauma will be reduced.

Overuse Injury

Many types of overuse injuries occur in cycling, ranging from knee and back pain to numbness of the hands or penis. As the name implies, such problems usually are caused by overuse of the affected part, but other factors can contribute, including abrupt changes in routines or equipment, sudden overload, anatomical variation, and inflexibility.

A characteristic of the body is that it needs time to gradually adapt to change. Abrupt alterations in exercise intensity, duration, frequency, or modality can cause muscular/tendon strain. Also, abrupt changes in equipment such as position on the cycle or saddle height can result in pain. A rider who begins to experience pain must evaluate its cause. Something is wrong and must be corrected. At times the problem can be traced to an abrupt change or sudden overload, but anatomical variations or inflexibility can be the cause.

Few athletes have symmetrical bodies. Often differences exist in leg lengths, arm lengths, or other body parts. For example, Greg LeMond has dramatically different foot sizes. Such anatomical variations can cause the overload of one area of the body, eventually leading to overuse injury.

As muscles strengthen they shorten, and muscles that shorten too much become inflexible and susceptible to injury, particularly when they are abruptly called on to perform. A flexibility program is an important part of any racer's training, as is massage. Stretching and massage help keep the working muscles supple, reducing the chances of injury. Stretching should be done at least before and after exercise, always slowly without bouncing. Muscles should be massaged toward the heart, helping to eliminate the waste products of hard exercise.

Tendonitis. Tendonitis is an inflammation of a tendon and its sheath. The normal smooth movement is lost, and pain results. This is often caused by overuse. Treatment of the acute problem involves the R.I.C.E. method described in the section on strains and sprains. Chronic tendonitis deserves professional evaluation and treatment.

Knee Pain. Knee pain is perhaps cycling's most common overuse problem. The pain can be the result of an abrupt overload such as a heavy training day or a difficult race, an acute problem that usually passes quickly, or it can be a chronic malady. Chronic knee pain can be caused by incorrect saddle position, chondromalacia, incorrect riding style (pushing gears that are too big—grinding instead of spinning), or incorrect shoe-cleat placement.

Incorrect saddle position, chondromalacia, and incorrect riding style are potentially related. Incorrect saddle position places stress on the knee, particularly the area where the patella and femur touch. When the saddle is placed too high, the biomechanics of the knee result in forces that try to drive the patella laterally or to the outside as extension is achieved, especially when the rider has a Q-angle greater than 10°. (The Q-angle is the outer angulation of the lower leg with respect to the upper leg.) Pain on the outside of the patella can result. This can be exacerbated if the rider has excessively pronated feet (flat feet). On the other hand, when the saddle is too low, the leg is bent too much, and the resultant forces put a great deal of overload on the patella/femur interface. If this problem is present for too long, and especially if the riding style is one of grinding big gears, chondromalacia can result.

True chondromalacia is degeneration of the cartilage that lines the underside of the patella. The cartilage breakdown causes pain beneath the kneecap and significant loss of leg function, especially leg extension under load. Fortunately, true chondromalacia is fairly rare among cycle racers. Many riders develop a knee crepitus (crunching) on extension, but most of them do not experience pain.

The cause of pain on the medial (inside) or lateral (outside) aspects of the knee is often found at the foot. If the position of the racing-shoe cleat points the toes in, the knee is forced in toward the cycle, and medial pain can occur. In contrast, when the toes are pointed out, the knee is forced away from the cycle, often causing lateral knee pain. If a rider is experiencing such pain, an adjustment of the cleats may be necessary, but such adjustments must be made gradually. Knee pain occurs for a number of other subtle reasons. The knees are complex joints, and chronic pain in one or both should make the rider seek medical help. Consultation with both a sports-medicine orthopedic surgeon and a podiatrist may be necessary.

Foot Problems.   Many riders experience numbness of the feet at one time or another, a problem caused by excessive pressure on the digital nerves. The solution includes fitting the shoes properly (adequate room in the toe box), not lacing the shoes too tightly, and not tightening the pedal straps too much.

Back Pain. Many cycle racers have low back pain. Often riders will take advantage of a quiet period during a race to sit straight up and hyperextend their backs (bend a little backward, carefully). Doctor Thomas Dickson believes that low back pain among cyclists is caused by the back's erector spinae muscles existing in a chronic state of isometric contraction during a ride, and an occasional hyperextension can be helpful. Also helpful are back strengthening and stretching exercises off the cycle. Most cyclists overlook the fact that the back is the link between the legs and the upper body. Strengthening exercises will utlimately improve performance.

Hand Problems. Rare is the rider who has not had numb hands at one time or another. Both the median and ulnar nerves can be affected. Problems with the former cause numbness of the thumb and index and middle fingers, whereas dysfunction of the latter can make the ring and little fingers numb. Pressure on the area around the nerves (median—the middle of the palm, ulnar—the area of the palm opposite the thumb) causes an ischemic neuropathy, and the subsequent reduced nerve function creates the numbness. If the nerves are not allowed to fully recover, muscle weakness and wasting within the hands can develop.

If sensation does not quickly return to an affected hand, the rider must not ride again until it becomes completely normal. Afterward, the rider should examine his or her position on the cycle, because an incorrect position can put too much weight on the hands. Prevention of the problem involves correct riding position, frequent changes of hand position, and use of cycling gloves.

Injuries From the Saddle. Exept when the rider is standing, the saddle is the part of the cycle that carries most of the weight. As a result, the saddle creates a number of overuse problems. The skin of the perineum (crotch) is affected by pressure, heat, and moisture. That combination can cause irritation, rashes, and even boils. Rashes and irritation should be treated with careful hygiene and perhaps a hydrocortisone cream. Boils often need to be incised, drained, soaked, and a broad spectrum antibiotic used. Prevention of such problems should focus on the use of clean cycling shorts. (Wash after each ride and dry in the sun if possible in order to expose the chamois to ultraviolet light; recondition the chamois with one of the many creams on the market.) Something like petroleum jelly on the perineum will help reduce friction.

The male rider can potentially experience urethritis, prostatitis, and a numb penis. Cycling urethritis is a sterile inflammation of the urethra that causes burning on urination, frequent urination, and dribbling.

Cycling prostatitis is an inflammation of the prostate gland from the trauma of riding. Its symptoms can include mild low back pain and pain in the lower abdomen. As with numb hands, the numb penis is caused by pressure that creates an ischemic neuropathy, with only sensation usually being affected and erection and ejaculation rarely involved. To correct these maladies, the rider must stay off the cycle until the symptoms are completely gone. The cyclist should then examine his saddle and riding positions and also consider changing saddles, all before returning to riding.

Injury Overview

All riders must have the prevention of injury as one of their goals. Several things can help in the achievement of that goal:

1. Be mentally prepared for a race. Inadequate mental preparation can lead to concentration lapses during the race, and the risk of accident increases.
2. Be physically prepared for a race. Inadequate physical preparation can result in premature fatigue during the race, and fatigue can reduce the effectiveness of various reflexive actions that might prevent accidents.
3. Be mechanically prepared for a race. If the cycle is inadequately prepared, accidents can occur due to mechanical failure. Also, an improper riding position or improper riding equipment can result in overuse injury.
4. Warm-up, warm-down, stretch. An adequate warm-up is necessary before strenuous exercise. The body needs to heat up, become prepared for increased metabolic activity, and the muscles need to be more pliable. After exercise an adequate warm-down period will allow the body to gradually adjust to lower levels of activity. Stretching is necessary to keep the working muscle supple. Stretching is best done after a brief warm-up before the heavy exercise, and after the exercise period. Warm muscles and tendons are more pliable.

If a rider does sustain an injury, several things can help in correcting it:

1. Treat the injury right to make it right. Many riders try to "ride through" an injury or ignore the proper treatment methods or attempt to hurry along the healing process. All of these errors in judgment can make an injury worse or prolong its healing time, or both.

2. Return to exercise slowly. When an injury is healed, a rider must slowly work back up to the previous levels of competition. Too much too soon can cause overload, overuse problems.
3. Listen to your body. Every rider must learn to listen to his or her body and heed what that body is saying. If something causes pain, do not do it. Self-knowledge is the most important factor in both prevention and correction of injury.

Environmental Problems

Hyperthermia

Hyperthermia is elevated body temperature. As a racer begins to exercise, his or her body's internal temperature rises due to increased metabolic activity and muscle friction. Core temperature can approach 40 °C (104 °F) or more, and the temperature in the working muscles can reach 41.7 °C (107 °F).

The body must get rid of that extra heat. Among the various mechanisms available for heat removal, sweating is the most effective. As the sweat on the skin evaporates, heat is removed from the body. If heat removal does not occur, problems can result. Heat cramps are the most common and least serious of the hyperthermia problems. They occur in muscles immediately following strenuous exercise. The treatment is rest, massage, and plenty of oral fluids.

Next up in severity is heat exhaustion. Its signs and symptoms are weakness, headache, profuse sweating, and fatigue. A rider experiencing these symptoms should stop immediately, cool down, and slowly drink plenty of fluids. Unfortunately, riders who refuse to heed warning signs can suffer heat stroke. This is a true medical emergency—the victim can die. The signs and symptoms of this malady are an elevated core temperature (41 °C [106 °F] or greater), disorientation, coma, and often hot, dry, red skin due to lack of sweating. Cooling of the victim must be started immediately, and he or she must be taken directly to a medical facility for treatment that can include rapid, monitored cooling, IV fluids, and medication.

Riders who fall victim to heat problems are more susceptible to the same problems for months after recovery. They must be careful when they resume training and racing. For all riders, acclimation to exercise in the heat is essential. This takes time. Training sessions of slowly increasing duration and intensity should be done over a period of up to 2 weeks. The rider should always be aware of the need for adequate fluid replacement, because dehydration can contribute to hyperthermia problems.

Dehydration

Sweating is like the double-edged sword that cuts both ways. The body can get rid of excess heat by sweating, but at the same time it loses vital fluid. Dehydration can result. A racer who loses only 3% of body weight through fluid loss is fine, but if 5% of body weight is lost from sweating, he or she is nearing the dangerous area. A loss of 7% or more of body weight from sweating puts the rider at great risk for problems. Extreme dehydration can result in disorientation, unconsciousness, and death in extreme cases. It also exacerbates hyperthermia problems. If a cyclist becomes thirsty, it is too late, because the thirst mechanism does not give an accurate picture of the body's state of hydration or dehydration.

Frequent swallows of fluid are necessary. Water is perhaps the best replacement fluid. As the body adapts to exercise in heat, it learns to conserve electrolytes. Even so, many riders choose to drink electrolyte-replacement preparations. If one is used, it must be dilute or hypotonic or it will be delayed in exiting the stomach.

Hypothermia and Frostbite

Winter training and racing have unique problems. If a rider is not careful, hypothermia maladies can occur, particularly frostbite. A cycle rider creates his or her own wind chill factor. This can cause excessive cooling of the body, and frostbite can strike the nose, ears, nipples, fingers, toes, and sometimes the penis. Those susceptible areas must be carefully protected. If an area becomes cold, white, and painful, it should be warmed up rapidly in tepid, not hot, water. Severe damage should send the rider to a doctor.

Medical Problems

With the exception of exercise asthma and diabetes, medical problems are rare. Even so, those involved in cycle racing should have some awareness of their potential existence, because several of them can be life threatening.

Sudden Death

Obviously, sudden death from exercise is unusual, but it has occurred. Autopsy studies of the unfortunate victims have revealed that the causes in younger people (below the age of 40) are primarily un-suspected heart problems, usually a birth or development anomaly or a fatal heart rhythm. Athletes over the age of 40, particularly those who start competition later in life, die mainly from heart attack. If a rider has experienced recurrent episodes of dizziness, weakness, pal-pitations, significant shortness of breath, chest pain, or syncope (faint-ing), he or she must be evaluated by a physician. These signs and symptoms can be clues to the existence of previously unsuspected problems. They must not be casually dismissed.

Exercise Headache

Headache is the second most common reason for seeing a doctor, and well-trained cyclists are not immune to the malady. Exercise itself can cause headaches. The two basic types are exercise migraine and benign exertional headache.

The exercise migraine was first reported in the 1930s by a runner, and it can exhibit all of the characteristics of migraines, including vision changes, nausea and vomiting, severe focal head pain, and more. The obvious problem for the racer with such headaches is to be able to ride. If the vision is significantly affected, it becomes dangerous to ride; a severe headache and/or nausea and vomiting can reduce performance. Riders who suffer from this malady should consult a neurologist. Some medications on the market help prevent migraines, including beta blockers and slow-channel calcium blockers.

The benign exertional headache is often less severe than a migraine. Unlike the migraine, the benign headache is usually diffuse and short-lived. Also, it can disappear as a problem as the rider becomes more fit. With rare exception, neither form of exercise headache is caused by serious problems within the head. If an exercise headache becomes steadily worse, the athlete should be checked.

Exercise Anaphylaxis

Anaphylaxis is an allergic reaction to some stimulus, and, unfor-tunately, exercise itself can act in such a manner. A rider can be allergic to exercise. A racer with this malady can experience nausea and vomit-ing, abdominal swelling, hives, swelling of the face, neck, or throat, wheezing or difficulty breathing, and even shock in extreme cases. The problem can present itself as a combination of any or all of these signs, and each episode can be worse than the last. Most importantly, breath-ing difficulties and shock can lead to death.

The problem seems to be loosely correlated at times with weather conditions and also has a shellfish connection. Many athletes who have experienced it had eaten some form of shellfish within 24 hr before exercising. A rider who has been having such problems should carefully check his or her training log for any obvious connections, avoiding them if possible. Medication for prevention of exercise anaphylaxis is available. They are antihistamines and can cause drowsiness. Even so, a rider who has this problem should seek medical help and use preventive medication if necessary, because it is potentially very serious.

Exercise Asthma

Exercise asthma is fairly common. Asthma is a lung disease that has three components—constriction of the small air passages of the lungs, swelling of the lining of those passages, and secretion of mucous into those same constricted, swollen passages. The result is increased resistance to airflow, and because of the anatomy of the lungs, inhaling air into asthmatic lungs is easier than exhaling it. Air trapping occurs. Lung function is severely diminished. The affected rider has a tremendous decrease in the efficiency of his or her oxygen-delivery system, and performance is affected, sometimes so severely that training and competition are impossible.

A rider with exercise asthma may have it from the beginning of his or her career, or it can develop later. The signs and symptoms of the malady can range from a cough during and after exercise to loud wheezing with shortness of breath. It is postulated that the problem is caused by rapid cooling and loss of humidity in the smaller air passages of the lungs as a result of the increase in airflow with exercise, conditions which trigger the changes of asthma in susceptible riders. This postulate is compatible with the fact that, for many cyclists, asthma is worse during cool, dry days.

One way for the rider with exercise asthma to prevent the problem is to avoid training or racing on cool days with low humidity. Obviously, this is not always possible, and so medication is often necessary. A note of caution: A racer who is competing on the national or international level must be careful with such medication. Because many of the drugs are on the banned list, the rider must work carefully with both a doctor and the national team. The medications most often used are cromolyn sodium, terbutaline, or an aminophylline preparation. Compounds of ephedrine or pseudoephedrine are stimulants and thus are not allowed by the international athletic committees.

Diabetes

Diabetes is a serious disease. Fortunately, it does not always prevent an athlete from competing, but a racer with the malady must remember that races can be long events. Diabetics become adept at adjusting their insulin dosage, but athletic competition adds an additional complexity to the regulation of the disease. The diabetic rider must be constantly aware of the potential of hypoglycemia after a long ride. A recent study revealed that even nondiabetic endurance athletes can become hypoglycemic during long periods of exercise (blood glucose dropping to 30 to 40 from a normal of around 90 to 100), but they had no symptoms.

The insulin-dependent diabetic rider with impaired glucose utilization capacities obviously has a greater potential for problems if he or she experiences a reactive hypoglycemia simultaneously with one caused by insulin. The symptoms of hypoglycemia include weakness, sweating, headache, rapid heart rate, disorientation, and even loss of consciousness. A diabetic rider should carry one of the concentrated oral glucose preparations while riding. He or she must also become aware of the characteristics of the disease because some of the symptoms mimic what happens to any cyclist during a long, hard ride.

General Problems

Eye Problems

Few riders wear glasses. Because glasses easily slip off, become coated with perspiration, distort peripheral vision, and can cause injury in a crash, riders who need vision correction most often wear contact lenses. As a result, the rider's eyes are unprotected and are at risk.

Constant exposure to wind can desiccate, or dry out, the eyes, resulting in mild soreness, irritation, and redness. When this occurs, the use of an artificial-tear product can help. The rider should keep in mind that the symptoms of desiccation can also be caused by infection. If symptoms persist following a short course of use of artificial tears, or if a discharge is present in the eyes, the rider should seek medical help.

Dirt or an insect can fly into the eye, at times with a great deal of force when the rider is at speed. A corneal abrasion can result. When this occurs, the affected eye will have a foreign-body sensation, often described as "a piece of gravel in my eye." Careful self-examination might reveal a small object on the cornea (the portion of the eye covering the iris or the colored area). Even if no foreign body is seen, an eye with a persistent foreign-body sensation should be examined by an ophthalmologist. Foreign bodies and/or corneal abrasions put the affected eye at risk for serious infection. One important note: If during the treatment of the eye a patch is placed on it, the rider must not ride (or drive) while the patch is in place. The patch results in a loss of binocular vision and a crash can result.

In the event of a crash, the eyes should be examined afterward. The rider should see an ophthalmologist immediately if he or she has blurred vision that does not clear with blinking, loss of part or all of the visual field of an eye, double vision, a "black eye" with severe pain, eyes not moving equally, an eye with a distorted pupil, or obvious serious injury to the eye itself or to the face immediately surrounding the eye.

Skin Problems

The most common skin problem affecting the rider is sunburn. Hours and hours of training usually give racers excellent tans, but a prolonged race during the middle of a summer day can result in sunburn, even for a rider with a magnificent tan. A first-degree sunburn makes the skin red and sore. The soreness may last for a day or two, and it can be reduced with one of the sunburn products on the market.

A second-degree sunburn also makes the skin red and sore, but an additional problem of this more serious sunburn is blistering. A rider who finds blisters should apply iced towels to the area for perhaps 20 to 30 min in order to cool off the skin. Initially, the blisters should not be opened because the fluid in them is sterile and the skin beneath them has lost its watertight integrity, thus making it susceptible to infection. If, after a day or two, the blisters are still present, they should be carefully opened, the loose skin removed, and the areas that were beneath them treated with an antibiotic cream or lotion preparation until they have completely healed.

Another skin problem is insect stings, particularly those of bees, wasps, or hornets. The rider who is allergic to such stings should have an insect-sting kit along and be knowledgeable about its use. Someone who is allergic to bees, for example, can go into shock and even die from a sting. The nonallergic rider should apply ice to the stung area periodically during the first day and watch for signs of infection—redness, increased swelling, more soreness, drainage.

Overtraining

All riders are at risk for overtraining, especially those who have not reached high levels of fitness. The human body is plastic in both the anatomical and physiological senses. As a result, it will adapt to recurrent stresses and, in the case of athletic training, achieve higher capacities for physical work through adaptation of both the oxygen delivery systems (lungs, heart, blood vessels) and oxygen use systems (muscles, etc.). Even so, the body needs time to make these adaptations. Exercise periods are the stimulus for change, whereas the periods of rest in between are the times the body actually changes. If a cyclist does not give his or her body adequate time to rest, particularly after a strenuous training session or race, overtraining can result.

The signs of overtraining can include, among other things:

- Chronic fatigue
- Chronic soreness
- Frequent injury
- Frequent illness
- Irritability
- Loss of interest in training
- Loss of weight
- Loss of libido
- Difficulty sleeping
- Rise in blood pressure
- Rise in resting heart rate

A rise in resting heart rate is probably the easiest way for a rider to monitor his or her training. If the resting pulse taken immediately after wakening in the morning is 5 to 7 beats/min higher than normal, an easy or rest day is in order. If a combination of signs of overtraining are present, the rider must reduce his or her training/racing schedule for whatever time is needed to return the body to normal. Once the various parameters have normalized, the rider must build back up slowly, monitoring him- or herself carefully. Therefore, a training log is almost a necessity for all cyclists.

Every racer should also keep in mind that different abilities result in different hard/easy exercise sessions. An easy ride for Greg LeMond could be much too much for an average rider, and overtraining would result. Each rider must learn to heed what the body says, easing training intensity and duration when necessary. Chronic overtraining can lead to detraining and loss of athletic performance, not to mention illness.

Nutrition and Drugs

All racers are concerned with nutrition. Food is fuel and, to extend the analogy, quality food is needed to supply high-octane fuel. The rider must take in adequate calories. Ideally, he or she will be at the correct weight (losing weight during the racing season is unwise). The number of calories consumed should be watched in order to maintain weight. During the middle of the season, this number can be considerable. The calorie-supplying constituents of food—proteins, fats, and carbohydrates—need to be supplied in the proper proportions.

About 15% to 20% of total calories should be made up of proteins. They must be quality ones. The body requires that all of the essential amino acids be present in their proper proportions at the same time. If not, the usable amount of proteins will be reduced. If only half of the required amount of one amino acid is present, only half of all of the other amino acids will be used even though they are present in their full amounts.

Fats should constitute 10% to 15% of total calories. Unlike the amino acids in proteins, only essential fatty acid exists, and thus the rider does not have to be so careful about fat intake. The balance of total calorie intake, 70%, should be composed of carbohydrates, preferably complex ones. If this amount is consumed daily, the body will be able to replenish its glycogen stores between exercise sessions. This will prevent chronic glycogen depletion, a condition that can contribute to chronic fatigue and poor performance.

Fluids.   Adequate fluid intake is necessary for the cyclist. Careful monitoring of weight can be a guide. If lost fluids are not replaced daily, the rider can become chronically dehydrated with loss in performance.

Vitamins.   Vitamins act as cofactors in enzyme reactions. They do not supply the body with calories. They are not magic nutrients that will increase performance. If a rider's diet is composed of adequate calories and quality food, he or she is not likely to need extra vitamins. If concern remains, one of the many once-a-day vitamin and mineral preparations on the market can be used.

Drugs.   It is a sad fact that many athletes, cycle racers included, look for things that will improve performance in magical ways. Drugs are often used with high expectations. No proof exists that drugs will increase athletic abilities. They do alter an athlete's perceptions, but such alterations do not improve ability, and they might be dangerous. Drugs tend to alter an athlete's feedback perceptions of his or her own body. Loss of such feedback (pain, fatigue, etc.) can allow the competitor to continue when he or she should not. Injuries and, unfortunately, deaths can occur. Drugs should be avoided.

Summary

Cycle racing is one of the world's best sports. The reader might get the impression from this chapter that racing is dangerous. On the contrary, the medical problems associated with the sport are relatively minor. Possession of basic medical knowledge as it applies to cycling will help everyone involved with the sport better correct problems that occur and, more importantly, prevent problems whenever possible.

CHAPTER 10

Sport Psychology and Cycling

Andrew Jacobs
Sport Psychologist for the U.S. Cycling Team

Winning is 10% physical and 90% mental. This cliché is often used by coaches and athletes to prepare themselves for competition. Although the emphasis in American sports has begun to shift toward a better understanding of the psychological and mental aspects of athletic performance, until recently little had been done toward understanding the importance of these factors. Competitive cyclists usually spend countless hours each week developing their physical abilities. They devote seemingly endless amounts of time to training on the road, on the track, or in the weight room. These hours of training are directed toward the physical readiness that coaches talk about. As to mental preparation, most cyclists are simply told to "psych yourself up," "be ready," or "relax and you'll do fine."

Although the psychological aspects of athletic competition have generally been ignored in comparison to the emphasis placed on physical conditioning, tremendous interest has begun to develop in the past decade in sport psychology. The desire to improve the athlete in terms of skill and ability has prompted researchers to identify and study the psychological characteristics that may have a direct impact on performance. Today, coaches and athletes commonly believe that success in athletics is directly related to psychological factors. Cycling is no exception. The United States Cycling Federation has recognized the need to assist cyclists at developing important psychological abilities and has begun to include a sport psychologist on staff at most training camps and competitions.

Sport psychology, which has been defined as the study and application of psychological principles to athletics and sport, originally began in the United States in 1918 when Coleman Griffith investigated the physiological and psychological characteristics of athletes at the University of Illinois. However, a void existed in the study of sport psychology in the United States between Griffith's research and the personality studies that began to appear in the mid-1960s. During this period, interest in sport psychology began to take root and flourish in the Soviet Union and Eastern Europe.

Athletes and coaches in Eastern Europe have been studying and investigating the psychological component of competition and sport for almost 25 years, and their results often speak for themselves. In such sports as swimming, gymnastics, pistol shooting, and cycling, Eastern European athletes commonly excel, due in part to superior psychological preparation. These athletes often begin learning specific psychological techniques as youngsters to assist them at all levels of competition. United States National Coaching Director Edward Borysewicz has commented that mental planning and preparation were included in his training regimen when he competed in Poland. Sport psychologists often accompany Eastern European teams to international competitions. In contrast, the 1983 World Championships in cycling was the first international meet where the United States team included a sport psychologist on the staff.

Attention Span and Performance

Over the past 5 years a large amount of psychological research has begun to appear in athletics, including investigations into the role of attention span in performance. Many investigators have concluded that attention affects both arousal and concentration levels. Nideffer (1976) found that two major attentional dimensions and an attentional control factor have a significant effect on performance. First, athletes need to be able to control the width of their attentional focus. Width is defined in terms of the amount and diversity of information being processed. In a situation requiring an athlete to attend to several different cues in order to perform effectively, the demand would be for a broad focus of attention. In contrast, a situation that demands intense, sustained concentration on one thing requires a narrow focus of attention.

Second, athletes must control the direction of focus. This characteristic involves the ability to have either an internal or an external focus of attention. Examples of internal attentional focus include making use of past race experience, anticipating when to make a break or sprint, and being sensitive to one's own body. On the other hand, reacting quickly and effectively to another rider's break and becoming aware of what opponents are doing in a race are examples of an external focus of attention. Third, cyclists need to be able to shift their attentional focus as the race situation changes. This involves the ability to shift from a broad to a narrow focus and/or from an external focus to an internal one, all in response to changing attentional demands in the competitive situation.

These attentional abilities are demonstrated in Figure 1. When the two attentional dimensions are combined, four separate attentional abilities will occur. One of these, *broad external focus*, is the ability to effectively integrate many external stimuli at one time. In a criterium or points race a rider needs to be aware of the location of other riders

GRAPH OF ATTENTIONAL ABILITIES

BROAD

BROAD INTERNAL FOCUS
Ability to analyze
& make decisions

BROAD EXTERNAL FOCUS
Awareness of the events
going on around you

INTERNAL ———————————————————— EXTERNAL

NARROW INTERNAL FOCUS
Awareness of one thought
idea or emotion

NARROW EXTERNAL FOCUS
Focusing in on
a goal

NARROW

Figure 1 Graph of attentional abilities. From *The Inner Athlete* (p. 49) by R.M. Nideffer, 1976, New York: Thomas Crowell Company. Reprinted with permission.

as well as the condition of the course or track. A *broad internal focus* is the ability to effectively integrate ideas and information from several different areas. It involves decision making and analytical planning and is necessary when planning race strategy. Cyclists who compete in match sprints need to be effective in this area because they need to plan the kind of race they will have to ride against different opponents. A *narrow focus* of attention involves concentrating on one thing—either externally on another rider or internally on one specific thought or idea. Psychological research has determined that the most successful athletes are best at narrowing their attention under pressure. For example, in the individual pursuit the cyclist will need to be able to concentrate on pushing him- or herself harder and harder throughout the race and often focus in on a goal—internally on a specific time or externally on catching his or her opponent.

In order to be successful, cyclists need to be aware of the different attentional abilities and should be able to shift from one focus to another. At a 1982 training camp for elite cyclists, 32 male cyclists were given the Test of Attentional and Interpersonal Style. The averages of their results on attentional abilities showed that they view themselves as effective at all four attentional skills and were strongest at having the ability to narrow their focus of attention when necessary.

Arousal, Stress, and Performance

A popular belief in the past was that improvements in athletic performance can occur by increasing levels of arousal. Coaches often prepared athletes for competition with emotional and arousing pep talks. The research conducted on arousal and performance has found that, as arousal increases, an athlete's performance will improve up to a certain level. This level is known as the *optimum level of performance*. When arousal increases past this optimum level, the quality of the athlete's performance decreases. This theory is known as the inverted-U principle (see Figure 2).

Conclusions drawn from the inverted U indicate that some athletes may not be aroused enough, while others may become too aroused or psyched up before competition, resulting in a detrimental effect on performance. Riders must identify what they need to do to reach their own optimum level of performance. Those on the left-hand side of the curve may need to use appropriate motivations to prepare for competition. If they are competing against a group of riders they regularly beat, they might need to think about a specific time for finishing the race. Here realistic goal setting is important.

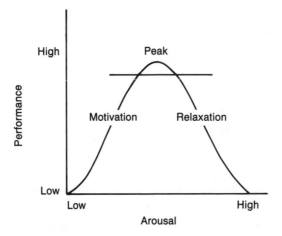

Figure 2 The inverted-*U* principle

Those on the right-hand side of the curve are past the optimum level and will need to apply appropriate relaxation techniques to calm down. Cyclists may find themselves on this side of the curve as a result of a wide variety of situations that cause an abnormally high amount of stress. Stress has become a popular topic in recent years. We need a certain amount of stress to get through a competition; however, too much stress will have a detrimental effect on performance. The situations that cause stress, which vary from rider to rider, are called *situational stressors*. Some examples are given in Figure 3. As they indicate, many types of situational stressors can occur, and these can change from cyclist to cyclist and from race to race.

A wide variety of physical and mental changes will occur in response to these situational stressors. The physical changes are generally associated with Selye's "fight or flight response" and include increases in heart rate, blood pressure, respiration rate, skin conductance, and most importantly, muscle tension. In other words, while waiting for the start of an important race, the cyclist may have sweaty palms, a dry mouth, a feeling of butterflies in the stomach, and may squeeze the handlebars a little tighter than usual. Mental and emotional changes include an increased narrowing of attention that can result in a reduced ability to analyze information internally as well as external events. This will be accompanied by an overall feeling of being rushed, confused, and overloaded. Additionally, the rider may lose his or her ability to shift focus of attention. This will result in an internal preoccupation with the physical changes that are occurring and will cause the cyclist to begin to think in a negative fashion and worry about the decrease in his or her performance.

Situational Stressors

Performing in front of family or friends
Racing against a rider of superior ability
Competing in a qualifying or championship race
Making a break in a road race
Running the last lap of a track event
Being the focus of a coach's or teammate's anger or criticism

Physical Responses

Increases in heart rate, blood pressure, and respiration rate
Increases in perspiration, dry mouth
Increases in muscle tension, resulting in muscle bracing and thus neck and shoulder pain, stomach cramps and nausea, and headaches

Mental Responses

An increased narrowing of attention, resulting in a reduced ability to analyze information and a feeling of being rushed or overloaded
Reduced mental flexibility as the racer begins to concentrate on attentional strength
Development of an internal focus caused by the physical changes that are occurring
Gradual increase in negative thoughts and worry

Performance Problems

1. Problems resulting from the physical responses include:
   - A gradual impairment in timing
   - A gradual impairment in fine muscle coordination
2. Problems resulting from the mental responses involve difficulty in decision making. Some individuals will become impulsive, whereas others become stiff or rigid. Specific problems include:
   - Becoming unaware of events going on in the surrounding area
   - Responding impulsively or becoming distracted by irrelevant thoughts
   - Increasing the chance for injury as a result of muscle tension and loss of concentration
   - Making a break or a sprint too soon

Figure 3 The effects of situational stress

Eventually, the physical and mental changes that occur will cause a variety of performance problems. Motor coordination and timing may become impaired because of muscle tension, resulting in uncoordinated or jerky movements. Increased perspiration may cause the rider's hands to slip off the handlebars. The lack of concentration accompanied by excessive muscle tension will increase the chances for injury. Additional problems may develop from the mental changes that occur and will cause difficulty in decision making. As a result, some riders will react in an impulsive fashion, such as making a break too early in a race, whereas others will freeze and fail to respond at all, always hanging back in the pack because of negative thoughts or second-guessing.

A situational stressor may thus cause various physical and mental changes that will have a harmful effect on the rider's performance. An example of this would be when a cyclist is competing for the first time in an international competition. Here the pressures of competing against world-class cyclists from many countries may cause the rider to doubt his or her ability. Consequently, when paired against the defending world champion, the cyclist may become so preoccupied with the opponent that the cyclist may forget the prerace instructions. As a result, when waiting for the gun to start the race, the cyclist may begin to notice tenseness in the neck and shoulders, shallow breathing, and a dry mouth with difficulty swallowing. This may cause the cyclist to wonder why he or she is competing against a world champion and will result in so much anxiety that the rider will be distracted by internal negative thoughts. As a result of the doubts and fears, the cyclist may fail to respond when the gun goes off (see Figure 3).

Treatment Suggestions and Applications

The first step in learning how to approach competition is the development of a mental game plan. At the beginning of the chapter it was mentioned that winning is 10% physical and 90% mental. What this statement indicates is that, when two cyclists of equal physical ability wait for the gun to start their race, the cyclist with the stronger mental attitude will most likely come out ahead. Once a race begins, a rider can do nothing about his or her physical abilities, but mental outlook will have a tremendous impact on his or her ride. Here the utilization of realistic goal setting is crucial.

Earlier the influence of the inverted-U principle on competition was discussed. The left side of the curve involves the use of motivation to reach the optimum level of performance. Motivation comes from setting goals. Thus goals can be defined as motivators used to reach success. They differ from cyclist to cyclist and competition to competition. For some the goal may be making the National Cycling Team, for others it may simply be finishing a road race, while others may want to finish in a specific time. Thinking about goals before and during competition can be an incentive to strive toward the actual accomplishment of the goal.

Realistic goal setting is important not only in competition but also in training. Every time a cyclist gets on his or her bike, he or she should have a goal. In training these must be goals the rider is capable of achieving. Training (or short-term) goals should be used as stepping stones toward obtaining the final goal or achievement. For example, a pursuiter who has as a goal riding a 4:50 at the National Championships, and his or her personal best in competition is 5:00, will need to set short-term goals. This might involve attempting to cut 2 s off the time at each race. Thus, instead of the pressure of trying to cut 10 s all at once, the racer will find it easier and will feel better about himself or herself by setting easier short-term goals of 2 s at a time.

When a rider is having a difficult time obtaining a goal, he or she must take the time to identify and assess the problem in order to design an appropriate treatment technique. Identification involves ascertaining the nature of the specific problem. Assessment pertains to evaluating the frequency and intensity of the problem. In other words, the pursuiter in the earlier example may have no difficulty riding a 4:50 pursuit time in practice but in races may not do better than 5:00. Identifying the problem is easy. The pursuiter is having difficulty racing and apparently is having the problem at all meet situations.

When the severity of the problem has been identified and assessed, a treatment program is needed to help the rider overcome his or her problem. The first step involves communication issues with him- or herself, as well as with the coach. Many athletes become nervous because of the fear of failure. Failing to reach a goal can often cause a lowered self-image and a negative thinking pattern. Fear of failure is especially common for younger athletes, who are particularly aware of the parental and peer pressure to succeed. In these cases, a talk between the rider and parent or coach can sometimes eliminate this fear. Emphasizing that champions like Greg LeMond and Rebecca Twigg do not win every race may be of help.

The field of sport psychology has applied several psychological techniques to athletic performance. The treatment modalities involve relaxation/hypnosis and visualization exercises. Their purpose is to assist the athlete in calming down prior to competition and in developing superior methods of concentration. Relaxation/hypnosis exercises are used extensively in all types of sports and exist in many forms. The masters of the martial arts are experts at concentration, as evidenced by their superior ability to relax and concentrate on the task at hand. Hypnosis, meditation, yoga, and biofeedback have all been used successfully worldwide in assisting athletes to further develop mental toughness.

One exercise that has been used with a great deal of success by several American cyclists is done in three phases. It should be done prior to competition, either the night before and/or immediately before the race. The first stage requires the rider to lie down in a quiet, comfortable setting where he or she will not be disturbed for approximately 20 min. The arms and legs must not be crossed and the rider must wear comfortable, nonrestrictive clothing. He or she should concentrate on taking long, deep breaths and continue this breathing pattern throughout the exercise. Next, the rider should tighten and loosen sets of muscles from the head to the feet, one set at a time. Often it may be advisable to repeat this twice, concentrating on the muscle groups that may be more tense. The muscle groups involved are the forehead, teeth and jaws, neck and shoulders, biceps, triceps, forearms, wrists and hands, abdomen, thighs, calves, and feet. The purpose is twofold: (a) It will assist the rider at relaxing before his or her race and (b) it may assist him or her in recognizing specific areas of the body that hold the most tension during competition. As a result, during the actual race, the rider may simply tighten and loosen these muscles to get rid of some of this tension.

The next phase of the exercise focuses on mentally relaxing the rider. After the muscle groups have been relaxed, the rider should picture him- or herself resting at a place that further enhances relaxation. Whether picturing a beach, the mountains, or other environment, the rider should be aware of how relaxing a place is. This will assist the rider in clearing his or her mind of negative thoughts or feelings. Finally, after the rider is both physically and mentally relaxed, he or she should begin to picture or visualize actually riding the race. Research in all areas of athletics has proven that visualization is a tremendous asset to performance. The rider can either picture the ride through his or her own eyes or as if he or she were watching it on a movie screen. An example would be the pursuiter picturing himself at the starting line, relaxed and calm, yet ready and focused on the race. After the race begins, the pursuiter should picture him- or herself on each lap and visualize what he or she needs to be thinking about and doing to be successful. Visualization is an exercise that should be continually repeated until the rider feels the way he or she wants to feel during the race, both physically and mentally. It assists the cyclist in becoming aware of physical tension, clearing his or her mind of negative thoughts, and instilling a positive attitude about his or her performance.

Perhaps most important is the mental attitude a cyclist takes into competition. If a rider approaches competition with a negative attitude, more than likely he or she will not ride a good race. The best method of learning from mistakes is to analyze what the rider did wrong and then change that failure into a success. The key to a positive attitude and intense concentration comes from belief in oneself through training and assessment of results. Road riders often talk about the difficulty of being positive throughout an entire ride. The riders who usually achieve their goals are the ones who can recognize when they are losing concentration and becoming negative and can change these around by using a rational mode of thinking. The 1983 United States Pan-American Cycling Team is an example. The team won seven gold medals out of eight events and broke several American and Pan-American records. The team was successful because the athletes were mentally as well as physically prepared for competition.

References

Nideffer, R.M. (1976). *The inner athlete: Mind plus muscle for winning.* New York: Thomas Crowell.

Nideffer, R.M., & Sharpe, R. (1978). *ACT: Attention control training.* New York: Wyden Books.

Index